Ray, to
readin   Nymay.

GETTING *it* TOGETHER

Noel Whittaker

To the young people of the world,
our future depends on you.

SIMON & SCHUSTER

AUSTRALIA

GETTING IT TOGETHER
First published in Australia in 1993 by
Simon & Schuster Australia
20 Barcoo Street, East Roseville NSW 2069

A Paramount Communications Company
Sydney New York London Toronto Tokyo Singapore

National Library of Australia
Cataloguing in Publication data

   Whittaker, Noel, 1940 -
      Getting It Together

      ISBN 0 7318 0387 6.

      1. Finance, Personal. 2. Young adults-Finance, Personal. I.
      Title.

   332.024

Designed by Carolyn Morgan
Typeset in Australia by Ocean Graphics Pty Ltd, Bundall
Gold Coast, Queensland, 4217.
Printed by McPherson's Printing Group.

ABOUT THE AUTHOR

Noel Whittaker is one of Australia's best known financial advisers and is a founding director of Whittaker Macnaught Pty Ltd, a leading financial planning organisation.

He is a pioneer in the field of consumer education and his books *Making Money Made Simple* and *More Money with Noel Whittaker* are international bestsellers. He writes weekly columns in many major Australian newspapers including the Sydney Morning Herald, Brisbane Sunday Mail, Perth Sunday Times and the Brisbane Courier Mail. He also appears regularly on over 50 ABC radio stations and often appears on television. He is in demand as a motivational speaker and has addressed large audiences in Australia and overseas.

His services to the financial planning industry were recognised in 1988 when he received the award of Australian Investment Planner of the Year.

He is married with three children and his hobbies are gardening and golf. His special interest is studying human potential.

ACKNOWLEDGEMENTS

When you write a book you appreciate the value of team-work. *Getting it Together* has developed from a combination of the efforts of a large group of talented and enthusiastic people who unstintingly gave of their time to help put the book in your hands.

A special "Thank You" is due to:

My wife Geraldine, for the hours she spent with me debating the content of each chapter. And to my children Mark, James and Elizabeth for putting up with Dad when he was too busy to play with them.

To my co-director Cheryl Macnaught for her helpful suggestions.

To Nicole Barry, Louise Beard, Lisa Bruce, Robin Laver, Carla Macnaught, Kylie Skillen, Chris Nebauer and Rebecca Nightingale (all from Whittaker Macnaught) for reading the manuscript and providing valuable feedback on the contents and cover design.

To Shauna Boyle, Roland Lindenmayer, Robyn Morrison, and Simon O'Halloran for spending hours proof reading the manuscript and making invaluable suggestions.

To Julia Cain from Simon and Schuster for her support and encouragement.

To Ron Tandberg for the cartoons and the fun we had talking about them.

To Carolyn Morgan and her staff for the cover design.

To Craig Padman and the team from Ocean Graphics for the typesetting.

To the staff of McPherson's Printing Group.

CONTENTS

INTRODUCTION

Since its release in 1987 *Making Money Made Simple* has become recognised as the standard work for people who wish to learn about the principles of saving and investing money. Seldom a day passes that I don't receive at least one letter telling me how that book has changed somebody's life.

I became used to the comments of "Why don't they teach this in schools" or "I wish I had read this when I was young" but slowly the feeling grew inside me that young people had a special need – a book written especially for them to show them where to start. After all you have to learn to make money before you can manage it.

The resolve to write such a book strengthened when I was at a 21st birthday party for the daughter of a friend of ours. During the evening I started chatting with a group of bright young people, the kind of men and women you would expect to be our future leaders. To my amazement they feared the future, were scared at the prospect of trying to find a job and were concerned about their ability to handle the challenges that life will undoubtedly present to them. I left thinking "If these young people feel like this what must the others be going through".

Soon afterwards in unrelated incidents two couples who were clients of our company suffered the trauma of having a teenage child commit suicide. There was no warning, or obvious reason, in either case.

A teenage suicide is a tragic waste of an important life and these incidents reinforced my belief that many of our young people are experiencing feelings of confusion and inadequacy. This is because they are trying to cope with the challenges of a new era that is dominated by technology and a drive for efficiency at all costs. While these feelings are understandable it is true that every age has had its difficulties and the techniques for personal growth and achievement that have worked before will continue to work now.

The aim of this book is to show you how to approach the challenges that lie ahead and to guide you into a success pattern instead of a failure pattern. The way to success is getting harder but those who are prepared will find there are boundless opportunities waiting to be taken. As the great inventor Thomas Edison said "If we did all the things we are capable of doing we would literally astound ourselves".

My wish for you is that you will approach the future with confidence instead of fear and that you will astound yourself at what you find you can do. The future of our world depends on it.

NOEL WHITTAKER

1

PUT ON YOUR RUNNING SHOES

When so rich a harvest is before us, why do we not gather it? All is in our hands if we will but use it.
Elizabeth Seton

You young people in the 1990's face a radically different world from the one in which your parents grew up. The remarkable technological advances in the last 50 years coupled with changes in social attitudes have given many people vastly improved living standards. Now we use television to watch events in living colour as they happen around the world, word processors have taken much of the drudgery out of typing, miracle drugs have improved our life expectancy, heavy machinery has replaced back breaking work, and discrimination because of gender or race is becoming less common.

However every action has an opposite reaction. Because computers and robots are doing a larger share of the routine jobs we achieve more output with fewer staff. Since women have taken their rightful place in the work force there is more competition for the jobs available. People are living longer because of medical breakthroughs and improved health care facilities. As the number of jobs shrink and more people join the unemployment queues those tax-payers left in the work force have to provide funds for a larger welfare bill.

The world is rapidly being transformed from an

industrial economy to an information driven economy. Production, administrative and clerical jobs will continue to vanish as the transformation goes on. To make matters worse our major businesses will not hesitate to build a factory off-shore if conditions are more favourable there.

For business managers now the buzz words are "Efficiency, productivity and customer focus". In simple language that says they want to look after their customers better but use fewer staff to do it. This means there will be fewer jobs available and more people trying to get them. The bad news is that it's getting tougher out there; the good news is that there are outstanding opportunities everywhere for those who become ready for them.

To take advantage of the opportunities that lie ahead you will have to learn how to make the right choices in your life. On the subject of the future you can choose to handle it in one of two ways:

(1) Complain about how unfair the world has become, give up trying and despair of ever getting anywhere in such a difficult and changing world.

or

(2) Take the situation as a challenge and make the best of it.

Certainly the world is changing and **you** face a different set of problems from those your parents and grandparents had to cope with. However remember they also had problems – they just differ from yours.

Therefore let's start our journey to success by your being aware that people have always faced challenges and that you are lucky to be living where you are now. Imagine if you lived in an overcrowded Third World country, or had been born to poor parents 200 years ago and were working in a mine or a factory at the age of nine.

While every age has, and will, have its own challenges there is another factor which you must accept. There have always been some who used the challenges as springboards to success. To do this they used some simple, universal and timeless principles which I will teach you in the chapters that follow.

I promise you these principles are **not** hard to understand and they will lead you to a successful life. All you have to do is follow them. That may sound a promise from Fairyland but it will happen. You are lucky. Most people never learn them and many of those who do, never make the effort to put them into practice. As you read you will come across names like Napoleon Hill, Og Mandino, Maxwell Maltz, W. Clement Stone and Denis Waitley. These are men whose writings have inspired the world and there is more information about their material at the back of the book.

Now might be an appropriate time for you to think about the two people who were hiking through the jungle when they heard the sound of a tiger nearby. Both were terrified but one stopped and started to put on a pair of running shoes. "What do you think you are doing?" said the other. "You know you can't outrun a tiger no matter what you are wearing on your feet."

"I don't have to outrun the tiger," was the response. "I only have to beat you!"

That's the way the world is going. The gap between the "haves" and the "have nots" will widen as jobs become harder to get and the work available becomes split more into skilled and unskilled. **You** can put on your running shoes safe in the knowledge that over 80% of the population will worry about what is happening yet will do nothing to improve their situation. It is the minority who will take action, such as reading this book, to change their lives for the better.

As this book is probably your introduction to the subject of success I have tried to make it an easy read for you. Most of the chapters are short and every one has one major message that is repeated continually to stamp it on your mind. At the end of each chapter you will have to decide if you want to keep on going or cop out. It's a bit like the TV game show where the player has the choice of taking the money now or coming back next week to win more. There is just one difference with this book – the chapters don't get any harder. If you can follow one you can follow the next.

Make your first choice now. If you are not interested in improving your life stop here and give the book to somebody else. However if you want to make the most of the potential you have, and the tremendous opportunities you have been given, put on your running shoes and read on.

2

IT'S NOT AN ACCIDENT

Every year I live I am more convinced that the waste of life lies in the love we have not given, the powers we have not used.

Mary Cholmondeley

The message of this chapter is that success in life is a decision, not an accident of birth or a lucky break. Your future depends on the actions you take from now on. What you have done in the past is of no importance.

You are holding this book in your hands because:

(1) Somebody gave it to you

or

(2) You bought it for yourself

If somebody gave it to you they must have had faith in you and thought that reading the book would give you some clues to a happier life. Congratulate yourself for being fortunate enough to know somebody who believes in you. That's a great advantage.

If you bought it for yourself it's probably because deep down you felt the itch of frustration. A feeling that life is like a beautiful valley that lies waiting for you once you cross the mountain. The problem is that the mountain looks forbidding and there are many well-worn trails at the bottom of it. You've tried a few that didn't go anywhere and you're reaching a stage where you are scared to try many more in case you discover that none of them will take you anywhere. That's how I felt for over half my life. You could sum it up by saying you've got a feeling you could really be something if only you knew where to begin.

Read on. This book will give you the clues to start you on the right path and to help you unlock some of that potential stored inside you. Congratulate yourself for being responsible enough to start to take charge of your future.

LIVING ON BISCUITS

We'll start with a story about an elderly couple:

They had lived a thrifty life but decided to have a final fling with part of the retirement cheque when the husband finished work. They booked a 14 day boat cruise but spent so much on the tickets that there was little left over for spending money. To overcome the problem, and to keep their spare money for shopping, they worked out a plan to save money on meals. They bought a large tin of biscuits and, instead of dining in the ship's restaurant, ate biscuits for breakfast, lunch and dinner in their cabin.

They got very tired of living on biscuits but the weather was great, the company was fine, and they had the best holiday of their life. On the final night of the cruise they carefully counted up how much spending money remained and decided they could afford to break out and eat their final dinner in the ship's dining room.

They got dressed up and prepared for a memorable evening. However when they arrived at the plush dining room they were puzzled when the head waiter escorted them to a superb table and handed them the huge menus because there were no prices shown. When they asked why, the waiter replied "Of course there are no prices – the meals are included in the cost of the fare!"

They had spent the whole trip eating biscuits because they had not realised the meals were included. What a waste!

Life is like that. **Most** people go through life living on the equivalent of biscuits because they never knew how much else was available. A fortunate few learn the lesson when they are young and some like myself do not learn it until they are 35. The majority never learn it at all.

SUCCESS IS FOR YOU

The message of this chapter is that success is available for you – **if** you know how to achieve it. Right now you may be thinking "It's all right for somebody like him to talk about success, he has never experienced the problems I have".

Let me tell you a little about my background. I was born in 1940 just as World War II was breaking out. My father managed a pig farm and I went to a small country school. In 1954 the farm was sold and we found ourselves with no home because we had always lived on the farm in the manager's house. My father was out of a job and the only place he could find work was as a labourer in a foundry.

I was so clumsy at school that the manual arts teacher would hold up my pathetic efforts at woodwork for all the class to laugh at. I was dropped from most of the Physical Training classes and never made a sporting team. When I finished High School I decided I was too dumb to go to University and, instead, joined the Bank of New South Wales (now Westpac) because it was a long-established institution and I wanted a safe job. For the first 35 years of my life I suffered with a massive inferiority complex and did not start to realise my potential until I read *Think and Grow Rich* by Napoleon Hill. My life was transformed from that moment.

The main reason I wrote *Making Money Made Simple* was to save people all those years I wasted. The reason for writing the book you are holding now was to get the message across to people when they were younger so they could put the principles into practice sooner.

You **must** understand that success in life is not dependent on what your background is, what has happened to you in the past, how brainy you are, how good looking you are or how much luck comes your way. Certainly people are born with different talents but **there is always a compensating factor**. Many gifted people find everything is all too easy at first and never learn the important habits of persistence and patience. Having wealthy parents can be a hindrance as proved by the problems faced by some of the children of so called wealthy and glamorous movie stars or members of the Royal family.

Many people from poor backgrounds discovered an unhappy home life provided the spur for them to do better than their parents. They may not have done as well in life if they had come from privileged backgrounds. Others learned from a tough background. The case of pop singer Billy Joel is typical. During World War Two his father was imprisoned in Dachau the Nazi concentration camp before migrating to New York where he found a job with General Motors. The family had little spare money and Billy Joel described he felt as if he was "A nothing . . . a zero in the suburbs."[1] Then his parents split up and Joel found himself with a mother who now had to go to work to keep the family fed. He recalls "it was traumatic not having food sometimes."[2]

Studies show that only a small number of family businesses survive to the third generation[3]. The process goes like this:

(1) The grandparents start to build a business from scratch. They pick up the necessary skills along the way and usually find most of what they learn is from experience.

(2) The next generation learns directly from the

1. Geller D. and Hibbert T. *Billy Joel — an Illustrated Biography*. 1985:7 McGraw Hill

2. *Ibid.*, p. 8

3. Benson B, Crego E, Drucker R. (1990) *Your Family Business. A Success Guide for Growth and Survival*. Business One Irwin IL. USA.

founders and, when the founders die, take over a thriving business. However the founders had the unique experience of building from nothing, whereas the second generation received help from their parents.

(3) The members of the third generation are born to wealth and are too often protected by their parents from the chance to learn. Because the grandchildren never had the chance to learn the skills of their parents and grandparents they are unable to handle the problems of the now large business and it may go into decline or be sold. The third generation often ends up broke and the cycle starts all over.

This has given rise to the expression "Shirt sleeves to shirt sleeves in three generations".

So forget about using your background as an excuse and remember that we all have potential we can put to use. In this book I will show you that success in life is predictable, and that it can almost always be achieved if you follow certain rules. Therefore there are two major steps; learn what has to be done, then put it into practice. You **can** do both if you **want** to.

3
SUCCESS — WHAT IS IT?

I want to be all that I am capable of becoming.
Katherine Mansfield

The aim of this book is to help you to become a "success". Therefore in this chapter we'll think about what the word means.

Becoming "successful" is a bit like becoming "happy"; the words have different meanings for everybody. One of my dictionaries defines success as "the accomplishment of an aim" and "good fortune". On his best selling audio tape *The Strangest Secret*, Earl Nightingale described success as "the realisation of a worthy goal"[1]. You will have to find your own definition but personally I regard successful people as those who are in control of their life, who are working at what they enjoy, and who are contributing to society.

Think of your life as travelling in a car. You can choose to be in the driver's seat, deciding where to go, how fast to go, and when to take a break. This involves planning the route, keeping a watch on the road ahead, and allowing for events such as hail storms, accidents or road blocks that may hold you up. You are also responsible for putting the fuel in the car and paying for the repairs. You

---

1 You will read more about this in my book *More Money with Noel Whittaker*.

experience both the pleasure and the responsibility. You are in charge.

You can choose to be a passenger in which case you will have no say over where the car goes; you will have to hope it travels in the direction you want to go. There is no need to look out the window or to plan ahead. You can stay safely inside and be at the mercy of somebody else's decisions and never have any say in your life. Whether you choose to be a driver or a passenger is up to you but, according to my definition, successful people are the ones who have taken control of their life and are living it on their terms.

Just be aware that it is possible to be a success in one area of your life and not in another. This is called being "out of balance". A common example is the business executive who works long hours but who neglects both health and family and spends most of the time suffering extreme pressure. The outcome is often a sudden heart attack coupled with the realisation, too late, that they have missed most of the true joys of life.

Success to me is :

(1) Working at a job you **enjoy** instead of hating going to work.

(2) Owning your **own home** so you are not at the mercy of a landlord who may force you to live somewhere else.

(3) Being able to afford to experience the wonders of our unique world through **travel.**

(4) Having **fulfilling** and happy personal relationships instead of living life in conflict.

(5) A degree of **freedom** to choose. It's a great feeling to go to a shop and choose on the basis of what you want rather than what you can afford.

(6) Feeling **good** about yourself.

(7) Having a **well-rounded** life so you enjoy a range of activities.

I promise you that if you follow what is in this book you will have a better life, you will be financially secure, you will wake up on most mornings looking forward to the day, you will have happy relationships and you will feel good about yourself. You will also discover some incredible powers within yourself. I am **not** promising you freedom from problems or stress but if you follow the principles in this book you will find they are a part of life that you will take in your stride.

GIVING UP TO GET

This is a good time to tell you about another important concept – to move forward you must give up. Saving for a home requires giving up spending all your pay for the security of owning your own home. Having children means giving up personal freedom for the joy of being a parent. Becoming an adult involves giving up being taken care of in return for being able to make your own decisions. A fit body involves giving up some of the fun of gorging on junk food. Owning your own business means you give up the security of working for somebody else in exchange for the chance to run your own life.

Giving up is a fact of life and none of us can change it. The good news is that you will find that by giving up you can achieve more than you had before.

In the next chapter you will learn your first lesson, how to avoid the negative pull of those around you.

4

MOST PEOPLE

We forfeit three-fourths of ourselves in order to be like other people.

Arthur Schopenhauer

The message of this chapter is that most people never learn or practise success habits and, as a result, die without using their potential. They often drift through life working at jobs they don't enjoy, dreading the thought of Mondays and yet fearing the loss of their jobs. They usually end up living on welfare convinced that life has dealt them a cruel hand.

In *Making Money Made Simple* I discussed the research that has been carried out on typical 16-year-olds. By the time they are 65, 76% are either dead or dead broke, 16% are getting by and only 8% (that's one in every 12) have made it financially.

That's a scary lot of figures but what do they say to **you**?

It should tell you that most people are doing it wrong. Now this is an extremely valuable piece of information – if most are doing it wrong it should follow that if you do what they do you will be on the wrong track too. Maybe it also follows that doing the **opposite** to what they do may be a recipe for success.

Earl Nightingale claims "winners do the things that failures aren't prepared to do" while Brian Tracy says that "Winners spend their time on activities that produce results, losers spend their time on activities that relieve tension".

Let's think about what most people do and don't do. I can tell you one activity they **love** to do. Most people waste at least 20 hours a week watching television and they **never** read books or take courses that will improve their mind.

They also can't wait to finish their work at the end of the day, can't wait for Friday to come, never set goals, and

spend their whole lives wishing they could win the lottery so they would never have to work again.

In a later chapter I will show you that our rewards in life will match our service, therefore it should be obvious that those who spend life providing no meaningful service to anybody else will get rewards in keeping with that effort. It may also explain why so many lottery winners who were broke when they won the money are back to being broke a couple of years after the big win.

"What about peer pressure?" I hear you say. "If all my

friends are having a good time, why can't I?" Hold it, I have never written anything that suggests people shouldn't have a good time. The aim of my books is to enable you to have the greatest time you could imagine by showing you ways to become more than you ever dreamed of. Believe me, the views are better from the house that overlooks the water.

Think about the quote from the German philosopher Arthur Schopenhauer at the top of this chapter and understand there is a time to resist peer pressure otherwise you will end up like the majority.

THE GREAT ESCAPE

I was one of the guest speakers at an Omegatrend convention in Fiji and sat enthralled as a high earning 24-year-old told his story to a large audience. He had been a shearer but found the work hard and the shearing sheds hot. His goal was to break out of those sheds to find a job he enjoyed and make more money. He told how he would spend night after night reading books like *Think and Grow Rich* and how the other shearers, who were more concerned with drinking, teased him about it.

His reply to them was "One day I'll be out of these shearing sheds and you guys will still be stuck here." The goal of a better life kept him on track and able to withstand the pressure from his workmates who, as far as he knows, are still shearing sheep and wishing they were doing something else.

Now I know it can be hard to withstand pressure from your fellow human beings but there are two solutions. You can either lead the group in the direction in which you want to travel or you can change your circle of friends to one that has goals and dreams that fit with yours.

Example: Mark wants to stop smoking, lose some weight and get fit. He has difficulty in getting motivated because all his friends eat junk food and drink and smoke too much. However if Mark joins the local gym he will meet people who are fitness conscious and will probably discover there is much more fun in going for a jog than hanging around bars drinking and smoking.

Alternatively he could do his friends a service and organise the whole group to go to the gym three or four times a week. Deep down they would probably all welcome this but nobody has got around to suggesting it.

I cannot stress enough the power of the people you mix with. People will respond well if you take them out of their environment (work or home), give them a good course with top instructors and teach them a bunch of skills. However the whole value of the course is generally lost within a few weeks if they return to their old environment and mix with the same negative people. The only solution is to send the whole group to the same course.

The reason for slipping back into the old pattern of behaviour is obvious when you think about it. It takes more effort to climb the mountain than to slip down it and usually the worst course of action for you is the easiest one. It takes effort to refuse a cigarette when your friends are having one and to say "I can't afford to go out – I am saving for a home" when everybody is planning a night on the town. It is far simpler to mix with people who have compatible goals with yours; then you can all agree to have a cheap night out or stay at home and make your own fun.

TAPPING IN

Another way to resist peer pressure is to be part of what Napoleon Hill called a "mastermind" group. This is a group of people with similar goals who meet with the common purpose of helping one another achieve them. Hill regarded such a group as so important that he devoted the **first** chapter of his famous book *"The Law of Success"* to the idea. He states he has proved time and time again that "every human brain is both a broadcasting and a receiving station for vibrations of thought and frequency"[1]. He believed the coming together of several minds created a mind that was bigger than all the others put together.

I don't want to spend too much time on the mastermind concept as this book is intended to be only an introduction to a new and exciting world for you. As you learn more about success you will find the concept of a mastermind group comes up regularly and as your awareness grows the right people will start to appear in your life. The point I want to get across is the massive power the people you mix with can have upon you.

It happens because we tend to act like those around us. If they are negative and always blaming everybody else for their problems they will drag you down too and you will soon start to act the same way.

Fortunately you will find as you practise the principles in this book that you will automatically move towards people who will help you get where you want to go. There is a Buddhist saying "When the pupil is ready the teacher will appear" and that has certainly been true for me.

Possibly the vibrations of thought that Napoleon Hill wrote about, attract to us the people we need. Maybe a mind that is prepared sees opportunities that are not clear to another mind. Whatever the reason it works.

Meanwhile don't forget that if you continue to act like the majority you will end up where they end up. Dead broke at 65!

---

1. From *The Law of Success* (1929) 1979 Edition published by Success Unlimited:47

5

STARTING A CHAIN REACTION

*There is no royal road to anything. One thing at a time, all
things in succession. That which grows fast, withers as
rapidly. That which grows slowly, endures.*

Josiah Gilbert Holland

In this chapter you will learn how to use a magic
formula to start a chain reaction that will take you
where you want to go.

By now you should know that success is possible for
you and understand that it **doesn't** depend on who your
parents were, how brainy you are, what you look like or
what you have done so far in your life. It depends on
your taking a series of steps which I'll call the "magic
formula". I have used the word magic because of the
extraordinary results that can occur once you start.
Actually there is nothing magical about it at all; it's
simply the laws of cause and effect operating.

Success depends on a chain reaction which, for you,
may well have already started. You take an action which
leads to a further action and then to another action and
finally you get a result that until now you may never have
dreamed was possible. There is one catch, the process
often takes a long time to work, which is why many who
start don't stick with it.

As Brian Tracy explained in his best selling audio tape

course *The Psychology of Success* many studies have shown that success is like baking a cake – if you use the right ingredients and mix them properly the result is predictable. You can therefore move confidently forward safe in the knowledge that if you follow certain clearly defined steps the results will come.

You are lucky because most of the research has been done for you. Napoleon Hill spent 20 years under the guidance of the famous industrialist Andrew Carnegie studying the techniques used by over 100 of the most successful men and women in the world in the early 20th century. They included Henry Ford the car manufacturer, Thomas Edison the inventor, George Eastman the founder of Kodak, and F. W. Woolworth who started the shopping chain.

Hill found that all these people used the magic formula and in 1927 published his findings in his book *Law of Success*. This was such a large book that he condensed the information into his famous book *Think and Grow Rich* which has been on the best-seller lists for more than 50 years. Every time I make a speech to business people I ask for a show of hands from those who have read *Think and Grow Rich*. Always a lot of hands go up and it becomes obvious that, for so many of the audience, Napoleon Hill's books were the start of their success.

Since then a multitude of books have been devoted to the subject and many of them adorn the shelves of my study. I have included the names of some of them in my suggested basic library at the back of this book because there is no doubt they have changed hundreds of thousands of lives. It is my heartfelt wish that *Getting it Together* will be the start of a journey for you that will include your reading many of the other fascinating books on the subject.

Now let's get down to work. In simple terms the rules of achievement can be summarised as follows:

(1) You must **believe** you have the ability. For many of you that will be the hardest part, but I will show you techniques that will put you on the right path.

(2) You will have to understand clearly that you must

make the effort **before** you enjoy the results. You may think this was obvious but you will find "most people" never understand it and go through life never making any effort and blaming everybody else for their failures.

(3) You must set clearly defined **goals.** Goal setting is what makes the major difference yet "most people" have never learned how to do it.

(4) You must **increase your value** as a person by continual self-development. This is a major factor because your rewards in life are in proportion to your skills.

(5) You must have **persistence** and **learn from your failures**. Failure is an integral part of success and it didn't stop you when you were a child learning to walk. How come you forget those childhood lessons?

(6) You must maintain a **positive mental attitude**. This is a habit that is easy to learn and comes naturally when you practise it for a while.

(7) You must take **full responsibility** for your successes and failures. If you can't do that you haven't got a chance because people who refuse to accept personal responsibility believe they have no control over their lives.

In the following chapters we'll think about each one of these factors and learn ways to put them all into practice. It's not difficult but it does take time and work.

As we proceed remember that being in control is one of the ultimate achievements in life. Think about it. The winners can spend most of each day doing what they choose to do – what makes them happiest. In contrast the losers spend most of their time worrying about money and doing things they don't particularly like because they have no alternative. The choice is yours.

BELIEVING YOU HAVE THE ABILITY

For many of you that will be the hardest part but the techniques that follow will help. The purpose of the chapter on self-concept is to show you how your brain works, to give you methods of changing how you see yourself and to make you think about what happened to change that unstoppable confidence with which you were born.

Look at any infant and you will see what **you** once were. Fearless, confident, curious about everything on the planet and with an insatiable demand for learning. No matter how often you fell over you got up again, no matter how much the adults said "Don't touch" you persisted. You really were a giant in the making.

Then slowly, and sadly, you began to take notice of "most people" and you started to follow the crowd. Your confidence gave way to fear and that thirst for knowledge slowly ebbed away. It became easier to conform than to be different and much more comfortable to stagnate while watching excessive television than to stretch your brain on a new skill.

The way to regain that confidence is to get it back the way you lost it – little by little. We'll go into it in detail in Chapter Seven.

MAKING THE EFFORT BEFORE YOU ENJOY THE RESULTS

You may think this is obvious but you'll find "most people" don't appreciate it. They want the degree without the study and the wealth without the work. Chapter Eight on sowing and reaping is all about the way our rewards are multiplied by what we put out.

SETTING CLEARLY DEFINED GOALS

Ask any winner what made the difference and they will say "Goals". Goal setting is of vital importance to success yet it is rarely taught in schools and "most people" have never learned how to do it. I have given it a full chapter in this book. If you follow the techniques you will reach a stage where you will be able to achieve any realistic goal you set for yourself.

PRACTISING CONTINUAL SELF DEVELOPMENT

This is a major factor because your rewards in life are in proportion to the way you develop your skills and as the world changes people with the right skills will be in demand. There is a full chapter in this book on the

importance of self-development, but if you "read between the lines" you will notice the entire book is devoted to starting a process that will bring out the hidden potential that is in you now.

UNDERSTANDING FAILURE

One of my major problems was that I never appreciated the effort that went into making a winner. I learned the piano for a few weeks but found it difficult and decided I must have no musical ability. Then I bought a saxophone and fiddled with it for a while but never got around to serious practice. I envied the singers and musicians in the movies who could belt out a tune with no apparent effort but got a rude awakening when I went to hear a well known singer and orchestra and made a request for a special number. They couldn't play it because "we don't have the music for it". That was the end of my illusions about ad libbing a tune as you see happening in the movies.

It wasn't till I was much older that I discovered that those who perform difficult feats with apparent ease have spent years of hard slog to get that way. Everything that is of value takes time.

Don't let the first defeat put you off trying again. To grow as a person, and to develop your skills, you must stretch yourself and try things you have never done before. You would be a most extraordinary person if you could get all these new skills right first time.

As Elbert Hubbard said "The greatest mistake a person can make is to be afraid of making one". There is nothing wrong with making a mistake and there is nothing wrong with failing. The only real failure is failing to try. Failure is an integral part of success and it never stopped you when you were a child learning to walk.

KEEPING A POSITIVE MENTAL ATTITUDE

If you have a positive mental attitude you expect the best from every situation. It's a strange quirk in life that we usually get what we expect therefore it makes sense to always expect good things to happen. Luckily it is simply a habit that comes naturally when you practise it for a while.

TAKING FULL RESPONSIBILITY FOR YOUR LIFE

The main message of this book is that you can have the most wonderful life if you decide to do what is necessary to achieve it. That statement implies the actions you take from now on will determine your future. As you have the power to control these actions it must follow that you have the power to control your future. Certainly it takes some effort but, as you will discover in the chapter on sowing and reaping, the rewards are far greater than the effort.

The author Bryce Courtenay wrote:

> It isn't hard at the top. It's easy. It isn't crowded and it's really quite civilised. What's hard is the bottom. Down there you'll find a hundred times more competition. Down there is where people stand on your teeth so that they can get a firmer foot-hold on the first rung of the ladder out of hell. Why then is it that most people seem so afraid of success that they'll do almost anything to avoid it.[1]

The choice is yours.

---

1. Courtenay Bryce. *A Recipe for Dreaming* 1992 William Heinemann. Australia.

6

REFRAMING
IT'S HOW YOU LOOK
AT IT!

*There is nothing either good or bad, but thinking makes it
so.*

William Shakespeare

The message in this chapter is that you live your life as you see it. Therefore you can change your life by changing the way you look at it.

You have probably heard the story about two men in a bar arguing about whether a glass of beer was half full or half empty. Of course both are right, it depends on your point of view. However, even though both are right, the person who felt he still had half a glass left may have been far happier than the one who believed that his beer was nearly finished.

As you go through life you will find there are few absolutes and that what you think you see is usually **literally** what you get. Because of this I will now explain a technique that has enormous potential to help you better your life. It is called "reframing", which means changing the way you look at something. It is one of the greatest ideas I ever learned.

Understand that you can choose how you think about something. How you think may be influenced by what you have experienced before, what you think you are seeing or how you have trained yourself to react. Here are some examples.

When I was a brash young 20-year-old I had just joined a golf club. One day I saw the Club President walk up to the first tee accompanied by what appeared to be a tramp. The man was dirty, scruffily dressed and to make it worse had trouble hitting the golf ball. Next time I saw the president I asked him why he was lowering the club standards by letting such a person on the course. His answer stunned me. "That man is a friend of mine who lost his wife and children in an accident about a year ago. His doctor thinks golf might help him." The moment I heard that I could have sunk into the ground, but it immediately reframed the way I saw the situation.

Years ago my wife and I were in Paris and I was operating on the premise that Parisians were very rude because they had seemed that way on my last visit. Naturally I had been rude back to them. My wife convinced me to try thinking of them as pleasant people and to act as if they were. To my amazement most of the Parisians we met were delightful. What had changed? Only the way my brain was working.

You should now understand that reframing involves you in thinking about situations and then making a conscious choice about how you will react to them.

Let's start with your reaction to unemployment, a topic that is critical to most of us. If 15% of people are out of work you will probably tell yourself that unemployment is 15% and focus on the difficulties that creates. You don't have to think like this. You could mentally reframe it and decide that, if 15% are unemployed, 85% of people must have jobs in which case there must still be plenty of hope. What if youth unemployment reaches 40%? Then is it not still true that 60%, that's nearly two thirds, of our young people **do** have jobs?

I'm not playing with words here. You have the choice of seeing it any way you choose. However the benefit of changing your thinking like this is that you start to get your mind **off** the worry of unemployment. This enables you to start focusing on ways to make sure you end up in the 60% that have a job, **not** the 40% who don't. Look around you and listen quietly. You will notice that "most people" waste their time focusing on the problem and never try to find ways to solve it.

You cannot change what is; what you can change is the way you respond to it. This will then change the way you act which will in turn lead you to a more favourable outcome.

I have introduced the concept of reframing early in the book because understanding it is vital to your success. Here are some examples for you to think about to make sure you understand it properly.

(1) *A young person breaks up with their boyfriend or girlfriend. The choice is to regard that as the end of the world and mope around for months or to regard it as an occasion to find somebody else. It may even be an opportunity to take an overseas holiday or find a job somewhere else that may lead to all sorts of exciting possibilities.*

(2) *A family goes for a holiday to the beach and experiences a week of wet weather. One family might sit around and complain about the weather for a week, another family might see it as a chance to go to the movies, play games and spend time together.*

In *Law of Success* Napoleon Hill uses the reframing concept without giving it a name. He states:

You are fortunate if you have learned the difference between temporary defeat and failure; more fortunate still, if you have learned the truth that the very seed of success is dormant in every defeat that you experience.

This means if you look hard enough you will find an opportunity in even the worst of happenings.

On the audio tape program *"How to be a No Limit Person"* psychologist Dr Wayne Dyer tells the story of the woman who was attacked, raped, shot through the head and left for dead in the boot of a car. By some miracle she survived this dreadful incident but is now blind. She laughed when she told him that now she does not have to look at her children's untidy bedrooms. I know this is an extreme case and she is showing a strength of character that few of us could match. However nothing can change what happened to her. She has had traumatic experiences which have left her blind for the rest of her life. Her only choices are to make the most of what she has left or to give up. She has chosen to look on the positive side.

You will see reframing everywhere once you become aware of it. Thomas Edison, the inventor of the light bulb, spent years trying to find the secret. Once a reporter asked him how it felt to fail 10 000 times – his answer was "I haven't failed 10 000 times, I now know 10 000 ways not to do it."

A friend of mine received a summons for $50 000 for alleged negligence. Instead of ranting and raving about having to fight the action in Court he took it as a warning that there were defects in his systems which needed fixing. Maybe that summons saved him from one for a much larger amount.

Then there is the story of two men who stopped at a news stand to buy a newspaper. The man behind the counter was one of the rudest people they had ever met. One of the men continued to be pleasant to the paper seller which prompted his friend to remark "How can you be nice to such an awful person?" The answer was "You don't think I'm going to let a fool like that control my actions do you?". Notice how he kept control of the situation in his own hands and how that changed the way his friend looked at the incident.

Our family now plays a game when we face a rude person. We put all our efforts into making that person smile and after a little work we usually succeed. I regard it as a great way to teach our children how to keep control of their emotions. Wayne Dyer tells about taking his family to a restaurant and being served by a rude waiter. Dyer said to the waiter "I can see you are stressed out – we are in no hurry. Why don't you take a few minutes to get yourself together and then come back to serve us?" You can imagine the effect on the waiter.

Playing "games" goes much further than having fun. By reframing the situation into a challenge and looking at it in a new way you are transforming yourself to a person who can take control of any situation. No longer are you a robot reacting mindlessly to anybody who wants to press your button – you have changed to a person who is able to control your emotions and take charge.

As you meet successful people in all walks of life you will notice that most of them have the philosophy of "That was meant to be" when an unwanted incident happens. W. Clement Stone the insurance company president greeted all bad news with the words "That's good" and then he would think about ways to find something good out of the bad that had happened.

When you reframe a situation you take control of it. By asking yourself "How can I turn this to my own good?" you are putting your creative powers to work towards finding a solution instead of wallowing around complaining like "most people" do. Suppose you apply for a job, or for a promotion, and miss out. The fact is that you have missed out and, for today, you can't do a single thing to change that. However you could analyse why you missed out and plan to do better next time. It is also possible that missing that opportunity allows you to take advantage of a better one that is waiting around the corner.

The ability to reframe a situation in a positive manner will be a critical factor in your search for success. In the next chapter we'll consider how your brain works and how you can start to think highly of yourself.

7

WHAT DO YOU THINK ABOUT YOU?

The greatest discovery of my generation is that human beings can alter their lives by altering their attitudes of mind.

William James

You now know the magic formula for success and understand the approach you take to life has a huge role in deciding your future. However knowledge is not enough. To succeed you must believe that it is possible for you. In this chapter we'll think about the key factor that will make you or break you – it's called the self-concept.

How do you genuinely see yourself? Ask a room full of teenagers, or even adults, and you'll probably hear a stack of self-derogatory comments. Words like "average" or "not much". Many will even take it a step further and use terms like too skinny, too dumb, too tall, too clumsy. There seems to be a feeling in our society that it's wrong to think good things about ourselves and it's common for people to tease their friends by putting them down in fun.

It's a pity so many people think like this because how we see ourselves affects almost every aspect of our life. This image of ourselves is called the self-image or the self-concept.

Remember in the last chapter we discussed how to reframe a situation to see it better; now we will consider reframing the way we see ourselves. To do this we will examine how the self-concept is formed, how it develops and how we can change it. This is a longer chapter than some of the others but stick with it, it's probably the most important one in the book. If you can master this, and it's not difficult, your success is guaranteed.

Our self-concept begins to take shape as soon as we are born and, sadly, for most of us it is a downhill cycle. We are born with a brain that is more powerful than the world's largest computer but, like a computer, our brain has to be programmed. We are not born with instruction books tied around our waists so "most people" go through life accepting whatever programs society wants to give them. Because we live in a world that is basically negative, most of the programs are negative too. This trial and error method of programming the brain with whatever happens to come along takes its inevitable toll and they go through life oblivious to what they might have become if they had only followed some simple rules.

Think of your brain as a roll of blank adding machine paper which is continually bombarded with messages from the day of your birth. These are stored till the day you die and your brain reacts to every situation in the light of what is stored in memory.

HOW A SELF-CONCEPT DEVELOPS

To help you understand the self-concept think about an imaginary person I'll call Miss X. She just happened to be born with a tall strong body into a household where the family tended to be big eaters and to eat a lot of junk food. Naturally she copied this pattern and developed the same eating habits as the rest of the family; her brain had been programmed since birth that this was a normal diet. Because of her naturally solid build and her bad eating habits she became quite plump.

Her mother, Mrs X, was also plump from the same combination of a naturally large frame and bad diet but she was always trying to have a figure like the slim models that featured in the glossy magazines she read. She was forever going on crash diets to try to look like these so called glamorous people but the diets lasted only a short while and she was back on the junk food path again. Miss X often heard her mother say "I've got no will-power, I just can't stick at anything". Mr and Mrs X often had violent arguments, particularly when he had been drinking too much, and Miss X would hear her

father call her mother names like "stupid" or "fat and ugly".

Miss X's brain was soon programmed with the beliefs that slim was better than plump, being overweight meant you were ugly as well as stupid, anybody from her family was doomed to be overweight, and furthermore they had no will-power. It got worse. Miss X's schoolmates teased her about being overweight and by the time she was 14 years old she regarded herself as a total loser – fat, ugly and stupid. That was her self-concept.

Contrast the case of Miss Y who was born with the same build in similar economic circumstances. Her parents knew the importance of good diet and taught her from an early age that she was lucky to have such a strong healthy body and that she should take care of it with the right food. The parents praised her qualities and never made derogatory comments about each other in front of her. From the day she was born she was treated as a special person by her parents and taught that, although life had its ups and downs, she was smart enough to handle whatever life dished up to her.

Miss X and Miss Y were almost identical on the day they were born but by the time they were 14 their belief in themselves was radically different. Why? Solely because of the way their brains had been programmed since birth. Their behaviour matched their individual self-concepts. Miss X saw each problem in life as further proof of her stupidity, Miss Y saw problems as a challenge and an opportunity to learn. Miss X reached a stage where she felt there was no point in trying, because anything she did try was certain to fail. Failure was her program.

You will read more about the self-concept in a later chapter about positive mental attitude but the above example should help you to know how the self-concept develops. The input from the world around you programs your brain and you start to act in accordance with those programs. These actions are in line with that programming and therefore reinforce it.

THE POWER OF WORDS

We develop our self-concept mainly by what we tell ourselves, by what others say to us and from situations we observe and take part in. Napoleon Hill tells how he regarded himself at age nine as a criminal in the making because his father had always treated him like one. Luckily his father remarried a great woman who reversed all the damage his father had done. When Dad introduced the young Napoleon as "the meanest boy in Wise County" she replied "You are wrong . . . he is a very alert and intelligent boy and all he needs is some worthy objective toward which to direct his very good mind"[1].

That was the turning point in Napoleon Hill's life. When, at the age of nine, he received his first compliment.

To further illustrate the point I will tell you something of my own life for in my experience it is the illusions of life that play a major role in fouling up our self-concept. As the song goes:

I've looked at life from both sides now,
From win and lose and still somehow,
It's life's illusions I recall;
I really don't know life at all.[2]

My father was a pig farm manager so naturally I was the "pig farmer's son". For some strange reason I got the idea that pig farmers were a lesser form of life than other farmers and I always felt embarrassed about telling people what my father did. My brother and I were never short of love or food but there was very little spare money. I have a vivid memory of the family sitting down at a restaurant called the Green Dragon in Surfers Paradise in 1950 (I was 10) and having to leave without ordering because our parents decided we could not afford to eat there.

Because I went to a small country school there was no opportunity to play much sport and my spare time was spent helping around the farm which I always enjoyed. When I got to high school I discovered that all those who had already been playing sport for their school went into the sports team and those of us who were left over were given a softball bat and left to amuse ourselves. This immediately produced in my mind two types of people: "sporting stars" who were in the school team with big badges on their blazer pockets and "the non sporting types" who had no sporting ability.

By the age of 14 I had a self-concept of being the pig

---

1. Hill, Napoleon (1967:11) *Grow Rich with Peace of Mind.* (Fawcett Crest, New York)
2. "Both Sides Now". 1967.

farmer's son who was too clumsy to play sport. It's an awful feeling to be the last one picked when the sides are being chosen.

I found my escape in books but the problem with the books I read is that they all starred the super hero that deep down I wanted to be. It's bad enough to feel you're a person with no sporting ability from a deprived background but once you start comparing yourself with all the heroes in the novels you are in real trouble. I did not know then that comparing yourself with others is one of the silliest things you can do.

My parents were ardent Royalists and Mum kept a scrap book in which she carefully gummed items about the Royal Family that she clipped from the papers. There's nothing wrong with that of course but it meant my parents strongly believed in a class system where the classes didn't mix. Apparently we were on the middle rungs and, for my own sake, it was drummed into me that people from our end of the ladder shouldn't try to climb up it much further. If we did try the unavoidable outcome of trying to rise above our station would be frustration and disappointment. Luckily they also programmed me that people from our station were "good honest workers". That program has stood me in good stead until this day.

I don't know where you're at right now and I don't know the background you come from. However it is almost certain that you have suffered much negative programming. Possibly your parents have split up and you are still feeling the effects of it; maybe you've suffered abuse or have been bullied or teased. Perhaps you trusted somebody who took advantage of you. Almost certainly you have suffered the insecurity of adolescence.

Actor Michael Caine described his teenage years like this:

> My nose was too big. The thinner you got the bigger it looked . . . These problems all sound insignificant to adults but to teenagers they take on an almost suicidal importance. Teenage children spend a ridiculous

amount of time looking in the mirror as their facial structure convulses, rises and sinks like a pot of boiling porridge. When all this is covered with a strategically placed veneer of pimples, you have the reason why most children never smile between the ages of 13 and 19. It is a terrible period for most kids.[3]

ADJUSTING YOUR SELF-CONCEPT

The self-concept does not develop overnight nor can you change it overnight. What you **can** do is start to make changes slowly and eventually the results will show. The following ideas will help you do it.

(1) Be aware the self-concept does exist and that yours has been programmed since birth. This awareness will help you to start to change it.

(2) Don't become angry about the negative programming you have received so far and start blaming other people for doing it to you. You cannot change what has passed and you are wasting time by dwelling on it. Everybody who has affected you was, in turn, affected by somebody else and it is as unfair to blame them for their actions as it is for somebody to blame you for yours. You will spend the rest of your life in the future which is where you should be concentrating your efforts.

(3) Be thankful for some of that negative programming because it may be a source of motivation for you. Some psychologists have referred to your negative experiences as the "burr under the saddle" that spurs people on to success. Frank Sinatra said "The best revenge is massive success" (that has kept me going on many occasions) and you can act on that by reframing your negative experiences with the words "I'll show them". As a friend of mine once said "Opposition is a help not a hindrance. Kites rise against the wind, not with it."

(4) Understand that your self-concept develops from what goes into your brain, therefore take great care to

3. Caine, Michael (1992:40-41) *What's It All About.* Random House

prevent any more negative programs taking hold. You probably haven't realised the main input to your brain is "self talk" which is what you say to yourself continually. A good example is what people say when they are playing sport. You'll hear statements like "My backhand is no good" or "I'm off my serves today" or "My putts are letting me down".

If you want to prove to yourself how the self-concept works, reinforce the other person's concept by saying "Yes – it's a pity isn't it?" and watch what happens. You could then try to help them improve by praising their good shots. Depending on the sport you prefer read one of the Timothy Gallwey Inner Game[4] books which show you how to excel by mental techniques.

Gallwey puts it "it was pointed out that the desire for improvement is natural, that man has a unique tendency to interfere with his own development, and that the primary form of interference is the forming of limiting images about himself and of trying to prove his own worth . . . Why are we so eager to accept beliefs about who we are, to identify with our performance appearance and roles."[5]

Exploring these ideas through books such as these will help you to become more conscious of the way your self-concept affects every action you take.

(5) Resolve that you will never again say anything negative about yourself. There is almost a tradition that we play down our achievements but I have never heard any of the real winners I know knocking themselves. If somebody pays you a compliment accept it with a simple "Thank you" and don't feel the need to add something derogatory about yourself to show how humble you are.

I met up with a friend once who I had not seen for many years. When I asked what he was doing he replied "I'm a

---

4. *The Inner Game of Tennis, The Inner Game of Golf, The Inner Game of Skiing* and *The Inner Game of Music* are published by Pan. They are all readily available.
5. Gallwey W. T and Kriegel, Bob. (1977:106) Pan.

Judge". "That's great" I replied. I was shocked by his answer. "It's nothing. I'm just a District Court Judge."

(6) Start going out of your way to help the self-concept of other people by giving them praise and encouragement and never knocking them. In a later chapter on universal laws you will learn about the law of opposites which states that you often achieve the result you seek by going in the opposite direction. Nothing will improve your own self-concept like helping that of others.

Never underestimate the power of your words on other people. I had words said to me when I was a teenager that still hurt today even though they were said more in fun than malice. Conversely I owe much of my success to encouraging words. I remember vividly walking out of Mass one Sunday morning to hear the parish priest Father Kevin Aspinall say to me quietly "I've been watching you, you will go a long way". I was 40 when that happened and the words came at a time when I was experiencing great self-doubt and inner conflict. Few experiences have given me such a boost.

(7) Establish a pattern of small successes and build on them. You will only harm your self-concept if you set yourself huge impossible goals after reading this book and then fail to achieve them. Our aim is to get you thinking like a person who can solve problems and overcome difficulties. Every small success you can notch up will give you the strength to go for a slightly larger one.

(8) Read as many autobiographies as you can. By doing this you will have the privilege of sharing the thoughts of achievers. You will discover they had exactly the same doubts, fears and bad programming as you have experienced. For example in Michael Caine's autobiography he relates how he believed that only handsome dark haired Americans could be film actors because he had only watched a certain type of American movie. This concept started to change when he discovered Spencer Tracy who was fair haired and not good looking in the conventional sense. He continues

"The clincher came when I saw my first European movie. It starred . . . Jean Gabin and he featured everything that I thought could hold me back: fair hair, a big nose, and a small mouth. He was the biggest star in France, so everything was now possible[6]".

When you read statements like that you will appreciate how your own progress is being held back by illusions.

A small book like *Getting it Together* cannot go into detail about ways to re-program your brain – there are many books and courses available to help you do that. The message of this chapter is that it is highly likely that you have low self esteem because of the bad programming your brain has received to date. When you have finished this book you will be well on the way to installing good new programs that will replace the old ones that may be holding you back now. At this stage it's enough that you be aware of the extraordinary influence of the self-concept.

---

6. Caine, Michael (1992:41) *What's It All About.* Random House

8

WHAT YOU GIVE IS WHAT YOU GET

or

THE LAW OF SOWING AND REAPING

There are 10 weaknesses against which most of us must guard ourselves. One of these is the habit of trying to reap before we have sown and the other nine are all wrapped up in the one practice of creating alibis to cover every mistake made[1].

Napoleon Hill

The message of this chapter is simple – we can only get out of life what we put into it.

Don't we human beings have strange thinking habits? We would **never** sit in front of an empty fire place hoping, by some miracle, that heat would come out of it. We know if we wanted heat we would find some dry wood, build the fire and then strike a match. Yet we are often guilty of hoping for many things in life to happen before we take the necessary steps to bring about the desired outcome. It's called trying to reap the harvest before we have sown the seeds.

Haven't you wanted top grades without doing the work, sporting honours without doing the practice, a fit body without doing the exercise? Of course you have –

1. Hill, Napoleon. *The Law Of Success.*

that's human nature. Ray Kroc, the founder of McDonald's, tells the story about a famous musician who was accosted by one of those chatty society women at a cocktail party. "I'd give anything to play like you," she said "No, you wouldn't," he replied. "You wouldn't be prepared to practise for hours, to give up the social life, to exist on a pittance while you were trying to make your mark – that is what made the difference."

The good news for you is that "most people" spend all their life wishing for things they haven't earned and only a few, that's right about 10%, make the effort to get them. Every Saturday night millions of people will be sitting round their television sets waiting for their "numbers" to come up. Sure somebody usually gets lucky and scores the big prize but many of those million dollar winners are broke again within a few years. In any event can you afford to let your future depend on a million to one chance? Your number just mightn't come up.

There are two rules you will need to know about sowing and reaping. The obvious one is:

(1) You cannot reap **before** you have sown.

The less obvious one is:

(2) You always reap far **more** than you sow.

Nature is clever. She knows it would be a waste of your time to plant a cup of corn if all you got back at harvest time is another cup of corn. No, plant a cup of corn and you may well get back bags and bags of corn. Better still, if you ate some of the corn and planted the rest those bags of corn seed you plant have the potential to produce thousands upon thousands of bags of corn.

In *Making Money Made Simple*, in the chapter titled The Torch, I tell the story of a poor boy, Orison Marden, who found out about the secrets of success in 1870 by reading *Self Help* by Samuel Smiles[2]. Marden became the founder

---

2. Samuel Smiles' book *Self Help* was first published in 1859. It was translated into 17 languages and has been one of the best selling success books of all time.

of *Success* magazine and Napoleon Hill was one of his first reporters. Hill then wrote *Think and Grow Rich* which has been read by millions of people and inspired the likes of W. Clement Stone, Jim Rohn and Og Mandino. Literally millions of people have been helped to a better life because the writings of Samuel Smiles sowed one tiny seed in the brain of Orison Marden.

Unfortunately the law of sowing and reaping works in both the positive and the negative. If you sow a few weed seeds you end up with a huge crop of weeds. Therefore the more "good" seeds you sow, the more "good" results you harvest and the more "bad" seeds you sow, the more "bad" results you have to cope with. What happens if you don't sow anything? It will be more weeds, not corn, that will pop up.

Good examples are the people who drop out of high school because the work is tough, try to find jobs to bring in some money and then make no effort to improve their skills. They bring on themselves a dreadful harvest. As a result of never gaining worthwhile skills they spend their whole lives in lowly paid jobs or living on welfare. Thus they cheat themselves out of millions of dollars of extra money they could have earned if they had made the effort to improve their knowledge.

Many years ago when I worked in the bank a teller "borrowed" a few dollars from the cash drawer. He was found out and the bank administration ordered his instant dismissal. It was only a small amount of money, and he had intended to put it back next day, but it cost him a promising career.

What excites me about sowing and reaping is the way small seeds can grow and the way a seed planted now can produce a crop many years later, often when you least expect it. This is why it is important to keep sowing "good" seeds all the time for you never know when they will suddenly burst forth into a bumper crop.

I made a speech several years ago to a group of car dealers and their staff. A new car salesman named Roy approached me and handed me his business card with the words "When you want to buy a new car give me a ring". I took one look at the card and noticed that he worked for a dealership that was 50 kilometres away. When I told him I always bought locally he smiled and said "When you have experienced my service you will buy from me". Some feeling inside me made me keep the card and six months later I was shopping for a car. I tried the local dealership but was put off by a rude salesman who told me an obvious lie by trying to pass off last year's model as a current one. That's one of the traps of buying a car in January – that difference of one month means a big difference when you come to sell it.

I gave Roy a ring, he sold me a car and has been looking after my cars since. Servicing is not a problem because he always has my car collected from home and provides a loan car for the day. I have referred many other people to him and I am sure they, in turn, have referred others. Just sowing that one tiny seed by the simple act of handing me a business card has given Roy a harvest of over 100 sales.

Many years ago I received exceptional attention from a young counter assistant in the public service and I was so impressed that I wrote a letter about it to the head of the department. About 20 years later I was negotiating with another government department about a matter that was of great importance to our company. Guess who was the senior public servant with all the authority? That's right, the once young public servant who well remembered the one time in his career that a member of the public had taken the time to show him some recognition and appreciation.

I could fill this book with stories like the ones above but I am sure you have got the message. Now you should ask yourself what good and bad seeds you are sowing and remember that many bad seeds take a long time to surface. Many of my friends and I now have problems with scores of tiny skin cancers that keep popping up on our face and arms because we spent too much time in the sun without protection when we were young; thousands of people die every year as a result of slowly destroying their lungs with cigarette smoke. **These were bad seeds.**

Most people reach retirement age without enough money to live on because they never "got around" to starting an investment program till it was too late.

You are young and have the opportunity to start planting good seeds now that will provide a harvest beyond your expectations. In the next chapter I'll teach you how to do it.

9

WHAT YOU SET IS
WHAT YOU GET

*What an immense power of life is the power of possessing
distinct aims. The voice, the dress, the look, the very
motions of a person define and alter, when he or she begins
to live for a reason.*

Elizabeth Strut Phelps

The message in this chapter is that the most extraordinary things start to happen when you set goals.

I was sitting in a plane waiting for take off when the flight attendant whispered to me "I wish I was in your shoes – look who is going to sit next to you". I looked up and there was the handsome form of ironman Grant Kenny. Grant turned out to be a quiet person as many high profile people are when you get to know them, but, as I had been studying success for nearly 20 years, I couldn't miss the chance to ask him what was the secret of his success. He thought for a second and said "Setting goals, I guess".

A week later I bumped into Kevin Carton who was then the Australian head of the Sheraton Hotel chain. Kevin is not just a successful executive, he was also an Olympic hockey champion. I asked him the secret of his success. Guess what the answer was. "Setting goals, plus the ability to keep a smile on my face when the game got tough – that really used to bug the opponents."

I have spent thousands of hours reading books and listening to cassette tapes about success and have found there is one factor on which they all agree. That is the importance of setting goals – the ability to decide what you want and then make a detailed plan to go after it. If you can master the art of doing that your success is guaranteed, for you have literally given yourself the power to design your own future.

When you set a goal you make a statement about something you wish to happen. However a properly set goal is much stronger than a wish, it's a commitment. Contrast this to the everyday chatter of most people "I wish I was happy", "I wish I could stop work", " I wish I could travel". These are not goals, they are dreams that will probably never happen. There is nothing wrong with dreaming but far too many resign themselves to the dream when, with a little effort, they could have had the real thing.

The moment you commit to a goal strange forces come into play and incredible things start to happen around you. It seems that once you set a goal your brain works on it day and night, even when you are sleeping, working out ways to bring it about and attracting events and people to you that will help to make it happen.

You can set goals in many areas of your life. Your goal may be to buy a car, have a holiday in France, lose six kilos in weight, buy a house, pay off a debt, win the local tennis championship, get a promotion at work or complete a study course.

Notice that you desire an outcome, to reach it takes some effort on your part, and that you will have to give up something to get it. If you are saving for a car, house or holiday it involves taking money from each pay packet and putting it aside. You have to give up the fun of spending now so you can achieve your goal. It's been called the icecream/ bicycle syndrome. You forgo eating the icecream today so you can have a bicycle tomorrow.

Similarly you must devote time to exercise and diet in order to lose weight, just as you have to put in hours of practice or study if you wish to win the tennis match or complete the study course. There is always something to give up. Notice how it all gets back to the law of sowing and reaping. Those who do not want to pay the price of giving up in order to get, finish with nothing.

SETTING GOALS

I'll now take you through the steps of setting a goal. We'll use the example of having a goal to buy a car.

(1) First you must clearly define exactly what you want. The brain cannot act on a vague goal such as "I want to travel".

You must have a clear picture in your mind of what the car will look like. This includes make, model, colour, number of doors etc. Find a brochure of the car with a photograph of it (coloured if possible) and stick it up on your bedroom wall where it will be the first and last thing you see each day. If you are choosing a second hand car you should be able to get a colour photocopy from car magazines in the local library.

Take a camera along to the local car dealer and have one of the staff take a photo of you sitting in the car of your dreams. Make sure it is the same model and colour as the one you want.

(2) Name the date on which it is to happen. It is no good saying "I want to buy a car". That's another wish. You must say something like "By January 20, 199X I will own a white Toyota Model XXX".

(3) Draw up a plan to get it. Suppose the desired date is 24 months away, the cost of the car is $9 000 and you have $4 200 saved up now. The difference is $4 800 and you have 24 months to find it. Therefore you need to save $200 a month. Can you do that? To find out you'll have to draw up a budget which is covered in a later chapter.

What happens if you do all the figures but the plan does not seem possible in the time frame you have set? For example you list your income and all your expenses and decide there is no way you can save the $200 a month you need. Now you have reached the interesting part – you must stretch your mind to try to find ways to achieve the goal. Ask yourself if the goal is realistic, even though it's a bit of a challenge. If it is realistic you will have to think of ways to find the extra money. If that's not practical you will have to modify your goals or act like "most people" and fall into the trap of buying it on hire purchase. This will cost you a large amount in interest costs which I'll explain in Chapter 20.

Let's imagine you are aware enough to stay away from unnecessary borrowing and the goal **is** realistic. You just don't have that $200 a month available. It's then a matter of cutting your spending or earning more money. Go over your budget and see what you can prune out of it. Are you buying lunches when you could be taking them from home, could you get a lift to work instead of using public transport, can you cut down on clothes, are you wasting money on cigarettes?

Now think about ways to increase your income. Is a second job possible, can you get a job at the car dealers washing cars and have the payment taken off the car price, do the neighbours need somebody to mow their lawn or to baby-sit their children?

The best part about learning how to set goals is the change that takes place in you as a human being. Once you think about achieving your goals you start to focus on ways to solve problems.

This is in stark contrast to "most people" who spend their life talking about the problems and never get around to find any solutions. By concentrating on the solutions instead of the problems you distance yourself from the herd.

You have now started to become a human being who has the ability to set goals, to make plans to achieve them and to adjust those plans if circumstances change. In other words you are starting to take control of your life. Congratulations, you are well on the road to success.

WHY GOAL SETTING WORKS

Goal setting works for two reasons.

(1) Setting goals gives your mind a focus. Think about what happens when your goal is to save for a car, you need $200 a month to do it and the photo of the car is on your wall as well as in your wallet. Sure you may be tempted to break out and waste some money but you will clearly understand that by having the "ice cream" now you will delay "riding the bicycle". You will also find the goal of owning the "bicycle" will become so dominant that the wish for the "ice cream" will be far easier to fight.

When my wife and I bought our home we set a goal to pay it off in three years. To help us stay motivated we kept a statement of the loan account pinned to the pantry door where it caught our eye every time we took something out to eat. That always kept us on track and the joy of watching that big loan come down gave us far more pleasure than spending the money on clothes or going out.

Recently we were visiting Tasmania and while browsing through a craft shop noticed a beautiful Huon Pine salad bowl with an inlaid pewter top. It was a magnificent work of art and we were both keen to buy it despite the price tag of over five hundred dollars.

We stood for over half an hour admiring it and fondling it. However our dominant goal then was to pay off a large loan we had on one of our investment properties so we could free up the money we were paying in interest to use for more holidays overseas. We finally decided to forgo the pleasure of buying the bowl because it was not in line with the goal of reducing the debt. The goal had enabled us to avoid the temptation. The price of the bowl was tiny compared to the debt we were paying off but we knew that once you start giving in to small temptations the goal loses its importance. You then fall into the trap of "Well, just this once" and it starts to happen over and over again.

If you have neglected an assignment and abruptly found the deadline approaching you would have experienced the power that comes from goal setting. Suddenly working on that project takes over your thoughts and you find a power and concentration you never experienced until the deadline drew near. You become focused on the task to the exclusion of all other thoughts. This is what goal setting is all about.

COMPETING GOALS?

The problem with setting goals is that you can become trapped among competing interests. You may want to buy a car, have a holiday, buy a house, buy a new outfit, get out on the town with your friends, take up the study course and win the sporting event. What do you do?

The solution is to try to put together a list of goals that will work together. For example when I was studying accounting after I was married I studied from 7 pm to 11 pm from Monday through to Thursday. This gave me Friday night and the weekend for other activities. Each study night I went for a 30 minute jog at 9 pm and followed it with a quick shower. This accounted for the exercise goal but it also gave me a bonus. The run and shower halfway through my study freshened me up for the rest of the night.

I also got a dose of motivation because I always jogged along the same route. Every night I would pass a house and notice the owner sitting in the same chair watching television. I told myself "In four years I'll have my degree and you'll still be sitting in the same spot wasting your life".

You could easily combine a study goal with a money making goal if you took on baby-sitting and studied after the children go to sleep. A goal to win a sporting event will usually combine well with an exercise or diet one. A savings goal will also combine well with a study goal or one to win a sporting event because you have to devote time to study or practice.

You must have balance in your life so don't neglect going out and having fun with your friends. Obviously if you are on a savings kick you may have to find cheaper entertainment but this often turns out to be the most fun anyway.

START WITH SMALL GOALS

This book is all about helping you to make minor changes in your life that will lead on to bigger changes later. Because you improve your self-concept by a series of little successes it is best to start off your goal setting

SMART GOALS

program with small goals that have a strong chance of achievement. Once you have mastered these you can move onto bigger ones.

For example if you have several small debts you may set a goal to pay one of them off quickly, say in three months. Perhaps there is a piece of sporting equipment you want. Set yourself the goal of saving up for it. Just practise the techniques I showed you of writing it down, stating a time for its happening and focusing your mind on it.

While you are doing this remember that goal setting is useless unless you take the right actions to achieve them. There is no point in setting a goal to buy a car in 18 months if you continue to spend all your money on clothes and entertainment; you are fooling yourself if your goal is to lose weight and you are still snacking on pastries and chocolates. Ask yourself "Does my behaviour match my goals?". If the answer is "no" you had better do some quiet thinking about where you really want to go in life.

Don't be frightened to use tricks to help you stay on track. For example exercising with a friend will usually make you turn up at the right time, leaving your credit cards at home will stop the impulse buy, and shopping after a meal will keep you from buying junk food. If I am writing a book I usually arrange the publication date first to provide me with a firm deadline to write to. Otherwise I fall into to the "I will start next week" trap, shuffle papers for months and never get around to doing anything of substance.

THE SALAMI TECHNIQUE

A variation of starting with small goals is to use the "salami technique" which gets its name because it is like slicing thin strips off a piece of sausage. You simply figure out what your goal is and then break it down into a series of small sub goals. Then each sub goal becomes a goal in itself.

I use this technique when I am writing a book because a book, like accumulating a million dollars, is far too big a goal to grasp. It is much easier to first make a list of the chapter headings and then work on the sub goals of writing each chapter.

In *Making Money Made Simple* I show the example of the ten step ladder to a million dollars. The ladder is only ten steps and the first step is to save a mere $2 000. "Most people" take one look at the million dollars at the top of the ladder, decide it's all too difficult and go

Getting it Together

back to watching television. The smart ones know you
can only climb a ladder one step at a time and focus on
the $2 000. When they have climbed that rung they move
to the next goal which is to accumulate $4 000. That is also
easy because it's only a matter of putting together another
$2 000 which they now know they can do.

It is in our natures to be encouraged when we achieve a
task and to be discouraged when we fail to complete a
task. By working on many small sub goals that combine
into a large goal we manage to keep up our enthusiasm as
well as finally accomplishing great things.

You now know what goal setting is and why it works.
Some of the books listed at the back will give you more
information. Now we'll move onto three essential skills
that will speed you on your journey to success.

10

THE THREE
ESSENTIAL SKILLS

Do a little more than average and from that point on your progress multiplies itself out of all proportion to the efforts put in.

Paul J Meyer

A s you know you will get out of life whatever you put into it – good and bad. This chapter focuses on three skills that will help you into a leadership role for it is through leadership that you can increase your opportunities.

My aim is to help you become a person who is in charge of your life and who can make things happen instead of being at the mercy of other people's whims. As Jim Rohn said "Either you are making plans or somebody is making plans for you"[1]. Therefore you should cultivate those habits that will transform you into a leader instead of a follower. Leaders are paid more, have more opportunities for self-development and there are more openings available to them.

There are three special attributes that will help you become a leader. None of them are particularly difficult, they don't need any special aptitudes and they are available to almost everybody. The big plus is that you

---

1. From his *Challenge to Succeed* Seminar.

can pick up these skills quickly and, when you master them, they will probably make a great difference to your life in a short time.

They are:

(1) Getting into the habit of going the extra mile.

(2) Acquiring some basic sales skills.

(3) Learning to speak well in public.

As you can see there is nothing too hard about any of them. The first is a habit which you should be able to pick up in a month and the other two are skills that are easily learned. Just don't underestimate the way they can change your life and, as you read this chapter, remember that "most people" never attain them. Consequently anybody who makes the effort to master them automatically goes to the head of the field.

GOING THE EXTRA MILE

Recently my wife and I were driving home from the annual Speech Night of my old school – Salisbury State High School, and we were pondering over the way fate had worked in that time. It had been 38 years since my first Speech Night at the school and I had returned to present the prizes and make a speech. I doubt if anybody in 1954 would have dreamed that 38 years later I would have been on the stage giving out the prizes but, against all expectations, it had happened. We tried to focus on what I had done right, as opposed to the hundreds of things I had done wrong, in those 38 years and discovered two factors that I am sure helped me along the way. They were going the extra mile and being a non stop learner.

My parents had instilled in me how important it was to always give of my best and it had always seemed sensible to me to keep learning and discovering new things. However it wasn't until I read *Think and Grow Rich* that I discovered that going the extra mile has always been the hallmark of successful people.

You see it everywhere if you look for it. I went out to my

golf club yesterday to practise on the driving range. The young assistant pro smiled as he threw half a dozen extra balls into the bucket and said "Better make sure it's full to the top". On the way home I crossed the toll bridge and, because it's my custom to go the extra mile, gave the toll keeper a cheery smile and a greeting. Naturally she responded in a similar fashion. "Don't forget you've only got one trip left," she said as she inserted the card in the slot. That's the way going the extra mile works. You put it out and you get it back. The beauty of it is that it requires no special skill, all you have to do is form the habit.

Consider the following incident. It is not earth shattering yet it has stuck in my mind since the day it happened and I have recounted it to audiences around the world.

The time was 7.50 on a Tuesday morning; I was staying at the Sheraton Hotel in Townsville. I was heading down to breakfast and was keen to pick up a copy of the Cairns Post newspaper because I knew it would contain a photo and an article about a speech I made there the day before. I said to the bell boy "Where is the paper shop – I am after a copy of the *Cairns Post*?". He told me the papers were sold from the small store in the lobby but it did not open till eight o'clock. "No problem," I replied, "I'll pick one up after breakfast."

I went to breakfast and promptly forgot all about it until five past eight when the bell boy appeared at my table with a newspaper. "Here's your *Cairns Post*," he said and disappeared. Now that's what I call going the extra mile.

Later I reported the incident to Elin Power who was the training manager of the Sheraton at the time and she told me the staff had been trained to try to outguess what the guests wanted and to surprise them in just the way the bell boy had surprised me. Now was that a big deal or not? It was only a small action and anybody could have done it. Yes it was a big deal, it is memorable and it causes a ripple whenever I mention it to an audience. That is because it was so unusual!

Contrast this to the case of a 16-year-old girl who came

to our office to do some temporary work. She was after a permanent job and, unbeknown to her, we were looking for a permanent junior. She was a good worker and would have been offered the job except for one bad habit. Every afternoon at 4.55 she was packed up and waiting to leave. That is the opposite of going the extra mile. She was never offered the job.

A friend of mine is an executive of a large company. He says "When we are hiring staff we look for the person who has done a lot of extra curricular activities while they were at school. **We don't want somebody who thinks life is a 9 to 5 job.**"

By going the extra mile you ensure you get noticed which means you will usually be first in line for any special jobs that come along. These extra jobs give you the chance to learn more skills, to show more of your abilities to others and to move faster and faster along the road to wealth.

ACQUIRING SALES SKILLS

Unfortunately far too many people have an image of selling as something cheap and nasty and regard salespeople as inferior beings who are not to be trusted. That's a wrong belief. Sure there are some shonky hard sell merchants about but most salespeople are honest and fill a vital role in our community. In most situations their role is to identify a problem, find the solution and convince the customers the solution is suitable for them.

Imagine you were considering an overseas holiday. You would expect the sales consultant in the travel bureau to find out where you wished to go, work that in with what you wanted to spend and then plan with you an itinerary that would suit you and give you pleasure. If you are looking for a new outfit the salesperson's job is to find something that you will feel good in, and that is within your budget.

In short, selling is the art of taking charge, knowing what to do and convincing others to take action. It requires similar skills to leadership. Good salespeople are among the highest paid people in the world because few will put in the effort that is necessary to provide a high level of customer satisfaction.

There's another reason too. The pay of most salespeople is calculated with regard to their performance. That's right – they are paid according to the sales they make. Most people would find that too uncomfortable but if you're serious about improving yourself doesn't it make sense to be paid what you are worth? That way you can earn more than others if you are good enough.

If you think about it nearly **all** highly paid jobs have an element of selling in them. It may be a doctor selling a patient on the idea of giving up smoking, a coach convincing the team they can win, a professor selling the need for more funds for the department, or a manager selling the employees on different work practices. Possibly it's a public relations expert selling the media on the idea of using a story, an author convincing a publisher to accept a book, or a parent selling the child on the idea of extra study. They all involve persuading another person towards a course of action that should be of benefit to that person.

Now don't confuse this with the idea of "hard sell" where indifferent or unscrupulous salespeople try to convince people to buy something that may be wrong for them just to make a sale. Yes, it does happen but you will discover those people never seem to get far in life because they are ignoring some basic principles that will be revealed as you read further. In my experience the dishonest hard sell salespeople make big money for a while but always end up broke.

Your local library will have many books on basic selling and your parents, employer or friends may have access to some of the good audio cassette tape programs that are available. See what you can find.

By developing sales skills you are learning to gain others trust, to ask probing questions to get to the heart of a problem, to handle trouble makers and to persuade others to a course of action. These are all leadership skills that will lead you to the top.

LEARNING TO SPEAK WELL IN PUBLIC

Do you know that most people would rather contract a serious disease than get on their feet and speak to an audience? Winston Churchill said *"The three most difficult things for a man to do are to climb a wall leaning away from you, to kiss a girl leaning away from you and to make an after-dinner speech."*[2]

It's hard to understand this fear of public speaking because most children love to perform in public. Apparently at some point in our lives we become self-conscious and start being concerned about making a fool of ourselves.

You will find hundreds of books about public speaking in your library but to do it well you need experience, a sound knowledge of your subject and communication skills. These are not hard to acquire. Knowledge of your subject will come automatically as you continue studying your chosen field and you can gain experience while you are learning communication skills.

The easiest way to start is to join a Toastmasters Club or Rostrum Club and become an active participant. At these clubs you will meet other frightened, and no longer frightened people who are all learning to speak in front of a group. Of course you will be terrified at first and it might help to think of the slogans "no gain without pain" or "the best way to overcome a fear of doing something is to do it".

Believe me it's well worth the effort. As each speech passes you will feel more at ease and the time will come when you look forward to standing up and holding forth. Then you will be able to help others overcome their fears as you develop your skills still further.

---

2. Reported in *"Idea Bank"* a supplement to *The Executive Speaker Newsletter*, October 1992.

Regard this moment as one of the many crossroads in your life – the road you take will have a vital bearing on where you finish. You can choose to think "I could **never** stand up and speak in public" and give into your fears.

This will make you even more scared to try anything new and may well deprive you of the chance to discover much of the potential you never knew you had. On the other hand you may think "I'll give it a go. I've got nothing to lose and everything to gain". Do this and you have just taken a big step on the road to success.

Think about it. We know that achievers do what "most people" are not prepared to do. If you make the effort to join a public speaking or debating club you have faced a fear and overcome it. Furthermore you have done something that most people are not prepared to do and have thus moved further down the path of self-development.

Remember: Not trying **guarantees** failure, trying gives you a chance of success.

11

FINDING YOUR INNER POWER

*Everyone has inside them a piece of good news. The good
news is that you don't know how great you can be! How
much you can love! What you can accomplish! And what
your potential is!*

Anne Frank

The message in this chapter is that you have many skills
that you have not yet developed. If you develop your
skills you will expand the value of the service you can
offer which will increase your rewards in life.

In 1978 my life changed when I went to a breakfast to
hear a talk by an American named Jim Rohn whom I
mentioned in the last chapter. I didn't want to go to the
breakfast because at that stage in my life I foolishly
thought I knew everything (after all I was 38 years of age)
but something inside me drove me there. The theme of his
lecture was "Don't wish it was easier – wish that you
were better". It really hit me.

Now if you are like "most people", and like I was at the
time, you have probably spent a lot of time wishing life
was easier. You have almost certainly wished you did not
have to cope with such ongoing problems as study,
finding and keeping a job, money, and handling complex
relationships with loved ones. That's a natural feeling.
Unfortunately you will find the problems don't vanish as

you grow older – you just get a different set of problems. Hopefully by that time you have learned some of life's lessons which may help you to handle them a little better.

Listen to the conversations of many of those around you. Notice how much of it is in the category of "I wish life was easier" and consists almost entirely of complaints about problems coupled with wishes that the problems would go away. Because the time of "most people" is spent thinking about problems, instead of finding solutions, their lives seldom improve.

However you now know about reframing and once you reframe your attitude from "wishing life was easier" to "wishing I was better" you can start to work on the skills that will make it better. When you do this you move the focus from worrying about problems to trying to find solutions. You can then start to take charge of your life instead of being a helpless victim in the control of others.

The solution to almost every problem is to educate yourself to handle it better. This process is called "Self-development" and means that you make the time and effort to learn new skills. This will help you in several ways:

(1) **New skills open up a new world of opportunities for you**. These include job promotion, a chance to travel and the possibility of starting your own business. When I read *Think and Grow Rich* I set a goal to be involved in my own business within 100 days. I was 34 and by this stage in my life had experience in banking, conveyancing, personnel work, accounting, tax, property development and marketing. These all combined to make me a useful participant in a building business and within 130 days I was in partnership with a builder. He brought his building skills and experience to the venture and we combined into a highly effective team. The time I had spent in self-development paid off.

(2) **New skills boost your self esteem**. Because you feel better about yourself you perform better. This makes you feel even better about yourself and you perform even better – so the cycle continues.

(3) **Your improved skills enable you to render a better service**. As your rewards in life will always match your service it must follow that by improving your skills you improve your rewards in life.

As a result of the years I spent working on improving my writing skills I now earn extra money by writing articles in several newspapers and magazines. Learning to type has enabled me to write faster and mastering the computer has given me extra time to write because much of my writing is done on aeroplanes using a laptop computer. It doesn't bother me now if a plane is late and I find myself sitting around an airport. I just reframe it to "Aren't I lucky, I have got an extra half hour in peace that I can use to write some columns. That will give me more free time when I get home to spend with my family."

(4) **Opportunity favours the prepared**. In every place of employment from the factory to the opera there will come a time when a key person becomes ill or unavailable. Then there is a frantic hunt for a replacement. If you are on the spot and have the skills you are likely to get the chance to show your talents. Do the job well and you are in line for promotion which is another opportunity for you to learn even more skills.

(5) In this modern and fast changing technological world you will fall behind your competitors if you don't keep up to date. **Continual self-development is one of the best ways to provide security because it ensures you are not being left behind.**

A MAJOR ENEMY

Think about this one quickly – "How much does a TV set cost to own?" You may guess a couple of hundred dollars a year but I believe the figure is closer to $1 000 a month. That is the money you lose while you are wasting time watching it.

Television is one of your greatest enemies because it provides little by way of self-development for you yet is a continual temptation because it is easy to turn on and even easier to leave on. The average adult watches over 1 000 hours of television every year which is the equivalent of almost **thirty** 35 hour working weeks. Just imagine where you would be if you spent 1 000 hours a year in self-development.

Television is fine for a little relaxtion but the problem is that many programs show an unreal world and serve to reinforce illusions about life. **Also the format of most programs is designed to appeal to the viewers with the lowest intelligence**. The result is that your brain receives little or no stimulation.

In contrast good books require some effort on your part and allow you to stop to think about the subject matter. They also allow you to re-read a passage if you wish. I have found reading autobiographies to be a wonderful source of motivation, as well as one of the best ways to improve my mind, because they usually tell of the struggles and the feelings of inadequacy the authors went through. When we read this our own troubles fall into perspective and we can be inspired in the knowledge that other people have faced and overcome worse problems than we have had to endure.

Books have the power to change lives. The book *Self Help* by Samuel Smiles provided the motivation for Orison Marden to rise above his poor background, put himself through university and then start the publishing company that employed Napoleon Hill[1]. Clement Stone credits *Think and Grow Rich* with saving him from bankruptcy and inspiring him to become a billionaire. In *More Money with Noel Whittaker* I tell the story of the business executive who saved his job, his health and his marriage after reading *Success Through a Positive Attitude* by Clement Stone and Napoleon Hill. This same book gave the famous author Og Mandino the courage to face life when he was about to commit suicide.

The great writer Aldous Huxley summed it up: "Every

---

1. The full story is told in *Making Money Made Simple* in the chapter titled The Torch.

man who knows how to read has it in his power to magnify himself, to multiply the ways in which he exists, to make his life full, significant and interesting."[2]

BE DIFFERENT – MOST WON'T DO IT

Unfortunately "most people" just aren't interested in self-development so if you take the time to improve your skills you will be in the minority. For example in 1979 H.M. Brickwell undertook a survey to find out why 99.5% of the 3 500 workers in a truck assembly plant did not use a special education plan their union had won for them as part of a new work contract[3].

In this plan the company was prepared to pay for any job related training – "training that can even include college degrees". Less than 20 people out of 3 500 bothered to take up the offer. Why so few? I have little additional information about the experiment but let's imagine what might have happened using our knowledge of human behaviour. The workers were probably in the low wage bracket because they had a low skill level and saw themselves as being trapped in that position because they were unable to pay for further education. Most likely they blamed their low income on their lack of education in the first place which was the fault of their parents who had not been able to afford to send them to college. They were sure their lives would change if they **did** have education and they convinced their union officials to fight for it.

Once they won free training they had a dilemma. Lack of money for self-development was no longer an excuse and they came face to face with the harsh reality that

2. Quoted in *The Books You Read* edited by Charles T Jones published by Executive Books, Harrisburg PA. Full details are in Appendix 1.
3. Brickwell H.M (1979) *A study of the tuition refund plan of Mack Trucks, Inc*. Hagerstown MD as reported in *Adult Development and Aging* by Rybash, Roodin and Santrock. Wm C. Brown publishers.

training meant study, doing assignments, attending lectures and giving up such luxuries as a few drinks after work and a night's TV watching. They now faced the real reason for being in a low paid unskilled job – their own lack of motivation.

Probably until then most of the workers had used "I can't afford it" as the excuse for not trying to improve their skills. Once that excuse was taken away I am sure they found other reasons not to try.

Why don't you stop reading for a moment and write down how much you spend now on such items as clothes, records, cigarettes, cups of coffee, movies and hair care. Contrast it to what you are presently spending on improving your mind. If there is a huge imbalance it might pay to consider that, in the long run, the money spent on self-development is what provides the money for the others.

self-development takes time and effort but, as I said in the chapter on sowing and reaping, the rewards always far outweigh the effort. Only by working on your skills can you bring out the potential that is bursting inside you.

12

FAILING – THE ESSENTIAL INGREDIENT

The freedom to fail is vital if you're going to succeed. Most successful people fail time and time again, and it is a measure of their strength that failure merely propels them into some new attempt at success.

Michael Korda

The message in this chapter may scare you a bit – it could also change your life. If you want to be successful you **must** expect to fail because **failure is an essential ingredient in success**.

Your reaction may be bewilderment. Right now you may be thinking the author has lured me into reading almost half this book, has promised me success, and now tells me to expect continual failures. That is true but the failures are ones that are going to help you to grow and to develop your skills.

Let's think again about what we are trying to achieve. We are trying to make you stand apart from the herd and find the courage to gain the success that is your right. To do this you have to take actions to improve your knowledge and skills – in other words to move out of your comfort zone. This means trying a whole host of new things that you will probably find scary at first.

These may include managing other people, handling difficult customers, taking up a sport, making a speech in public, undertaking a study course, or starting a business.

I remember vividly the time of departure when I made my first lecture tour on the cruise ship *Oriana*. It was June 1985 and I stood alone at dusk on the rear deck looking

out as the great white ship left Circular Quay and slowly reversed until its stern was almost under Sydney Harbour Bridge. Then it blew its whistle and slowly edged towards Sydney Heads accompanied by several tugs. The decks were crowded and everybody but me seemed to be with somebody else.

I did not know a soul and there are few occasions in my

life when I have felt so scared and so lonely. The usual silly negative thoughts ran through my head – "What if nobody wants to come to my finance lectures?" "What if those who do come don't like the lectures?" None of these fears came true and the trip was a great success. The point I am making is that even though I was 45 and an experienced speaker and traveller I was still plagued with worries. I am telling you about it here so you won't feel bad if you experience doubts and fears before trying a new experience. It's a natural feeling but it almost always goes away once you start getting involved in what has to be done.

The only way to become competent in the area you choose is to learn about it and try to do it. Now, unless you are an exceptional person, you are not going to get it right first time. Even if you did get it right first time by some stroke of luck or genius you would learn little by it – a real learning experience comes when it all goes wrong. It will be just like when you started to learn to walk, you tried many times, you fell over many times but you never gave up. You kept on going and finally you made it. Sure it was tough but if you had not kept going you would be lying in that cot today thinking "I would love to be able to walk but if I try I might fall over and that might hurt. It's easier to stay here where it is safe and comfortable".

FINDING THE GOOD IN THE BAD

In all his books Napoleon Hill has stressed that every failure contains the seeds of a greater success. In her best selling book *Pathfinders* Gail Sheehy points out that successful people are **not** those who have been insulated from failure, they are people who have **faced** and **overcome** failure. She notes "Repeated to a striking degree in the histories of the **most satisfied** adults was a history of a troubled period during childhood or adolescence when many rated themselves as very unhappy. Some hit close to rock bottom . . . Although an unhappy childhood is not something to be wished on anyone, those who struggle through it evidently do develop important personality skills".[1]

The possibility of a good outcome arising from a failure may be harder for young people to grasp than it is for us older ones because life is a bit like a novel – it takes time for the reader to see how the plot develops. Those of us who have been around for a few years have had the time to watch events unfolding. Let me give you three events in my own life to explain what I mean.

When I was 29 I worked for a law firm. One day there was an argument at work and I resigned in a state of temper. It was November and I was shocked to find that this is a time of the year when few companies hire new staff; they usually do it in January and February so they don't have to pay people over the Christmas break. After weeks of job hunting, and a few weeks of temporary work in a factory doing process work, I finally made the short list for a job that I was very keen to get – it was for a credit manager at a building company.

A week later when the "we regret your application was unsuccessful" letter arrived I leaned against the refrigerator and cried my eyes out for about an hour. I was devastated then but now, when I look back on my life, I can see that if I had got the job I would not be where I am now. Another job came my way a few weeks later that led to far more exciting opportunities.

In 1979 I went through a divorce and suffered all the pain and self doubt that divorce usually entails. I had a few female friends to go out with but there was nobody who looked liked being a contender for the love of my life. On April 1, 1979 I had arranged to go to a function with one of them but she rang to say she had "a better offer" and our date was off. Naturally I wasn't happy about being stood up but used the occasion to go on my own to a National Heart Foundation luncheon where I met a young lady named Geraldine who **was** (and is) the

1. Sheehy, Gail. *Pathfinders* 1981:60.61 Bantam.

love of my life. We are now happily married and have three beautiful children – Mark, James and Elizabeth.

In 1986 I got involved in a property development venture that turned terribly sour. By the time we had worked our way through the problems I had lost almost half of the material assets I had spent 46 years accumulating. In money terms the price was huge but what I learned in that venture has enabled me to make more than I lost. I must confess it was a frightening experience but I used the technique of reframing to help me cope. I told myself it would have been much worse if one of my family had become critically ill or had been killed. Looking back I can honestly say I got more out of it than the price I paid for the "lesson".

Certainly it can be hard to handle unhappy experiences and projects that turn bad on us but it is the most effective way we can learn. Just as a piece of iron is made hard by being plunged red hot into a tub of cold water so a person is made tough by facing and overcoming set-backs and problems. You will never reach your potential if you try to dodge life's challenges by avoiding new experiences.

GETTING THE MOST OUT OF YOUR MISTAKES

You will find that life continually sets you exams to find out what you have learned. If you fail an exam you are doomed to repeat the lesson until you know it. To get the most out of your set-backs try the following:

(1) Analyse the situation and try to find out what went wrong. When you are doing this be strictly honest with yourself and don't fall into the habit of blaming others for the mishap. If you have been fired from your last three jobs or you are unable to have a compatible relationship with another person it is likely the problem lies within you. Once you can face that instead of trying to camouflage the reality by blaming others you are well on the way to finding permanent solutions.

(2) Practise the technique of reframing and tell yourself

that what happened was obviously meant to be. Ask yourself if the incident has shown you a new direction. For example if a job application is rejected think about whether you may be better suited to something else.

(3) Set out to find something good about the situation. For example if you are booked for speeding treat the incident as a warning that your driving habits need attention and be thankful you were not involved in a serious accident.

(4) Treat it as an opportunity to re-assess your goals. Does this mean some of your goals are unrealistic or is the problem simply a minor detour on your path to success. For example if you fail to gain admission to the tertiary institution of your choice you may have to consider alternative routes to get where you want to go.

(5) Be aware that failure is only a temporary condition and there are many roads leading to where you want to go. Never forget the following statement by United States President Calvin Coolidge:

Nothing in the world can take the place of persistence.
Talent will not; nothing is more common than unsuccessful men with talent.
Genius will not; unrewarded genius is almost a proverb.
Education will not; the world is full of educated derelicts.
Persistence and determination alone are omnipotent.
The words "press on" have always solved the problems of the human race.

I have had it hanging in my office since I discovered it in 1976 and it has often given me comfort when the going got rough.

While you must accept failure if you are to succeed it is also true that you need to set up a series of successes to boost your self esteem and put you on a success path. Therefore, while it is important that you try new things it is also vital that you don't put too great a burden on yourself by setting yourself almost impossible tasks. If you keep at it you will soon learn the difference.

13

POSITIVE MENTAL ATTITUDE

Life is a self fulfilling prophecy; you won't necessarily get what you want in life, but in the long run you usually get what you expect.

Denis Waitley

People with a positive mental attitude expect the best for themselves and other people in all situations. In this chapter you will learn about the importance of keeping a positive mental attitude and why it has such a big effect on the way your future turns out.

The problem with the term "Positive Mental Attitude" (PMA) is that many cynical people see it as sheer foolishness. They get a mental picture of a couple dancing for joy as they watch their house burning down with their family trapped inside it. This attitude towards PMA may be reinforced if you attend some of the sales meetings I have addressed and see people mouthing all kinds of optimistic slogans which, deep down, they don't believe. They leave making positive noises, but never get around to doing what needs to be done to make their lives successful.

Norman Vincent Peale the author of *The Amazing Results of Positive Thinking* explained it: "Positive thinkers do not refuse to **recognise** the negative, they refuse to **dwell** on it. Positive thinking is a form of thought which habitually looks for the best results from the worst conditions. It is possible to look for something to build on; it is possible to expect the best for yourself even though things look bad. And the remarkable fact is that when you seek good, you are very likely to find it."[1]

There is a well known story about the two salespeople who went to a remote part of Africa in search of new markets. One reported there were no prospects of developing business because nobody wore shoes. The

other cabled "We have a massive untapped market – nobody wears shoes yet."

In simple terms if you have a positive mental attitude you are an optimist who looks on the bright side of life and who expects most of the situations you face in life to have a favourable outcome. **But**! What if the initial

1. Peale, Norman Vincent. *The Amazing Results of Positive Thinking* Reissued 1991:9 Cedar

outcome is unexpected, as it often is? Having PMA means you have faith that somehow the final outcome will still be a good one.

Notice how it is closely tied in to the material in the last few chapters. You can now reframe an unexpected result to put a good face on it. You know that failure is a vital ingredient in your success and you understand that every failure carries the seed of a greater success if you can find it. Once you combine that knowledge with the power of positive thinking you can take action to produce the effect you want or to adjust your goals to go for a different outcome that will still be favourable to you.

I believe that having a positive mental attitude is a natural state because I have never seen a baby that didn't have a positive outlook on life. However we seem to lose it as we get older because we become conditioned by the generally negative world around us. Because "most people" don't make it, they create a world where they will be comfortable. This is why newspapers and radio and TV stations prefer bad news to good news and feature the small number of bad things that happen. There is generally a headline on bad economic news or a disaster overseas, details of a car smash or a story about a murder.

You have probably noticed the ways the media tends to reframe all news to the negative, which is why the headline will be "Unemployment hits 10%" and not "90% of people still have jobs".

A DEPRESSION IS COMING!

On one of his audio tapes US Senator Ed Foreman tells the story of the young architect who had just won a big contract. He went to a restaurant to have lunch to celebrate but as he sat down saw a newspaper on the next table. The huge headlines were "Depression predicted". He got such a shock that he cancelled his meal. When the proprietor asked the reason for the sudden change of heart he replied "Look at the headlines – there is a depression coming. I had better save my money".

The restaurant owner was so surprised that he rang his wife immediately and said "There's a depression coming. Cancel that new dress you have ordered". The wife promptly telephoned the dress shop owner and told her that she had to cancel the order because there was a depression on the way. Naturally this worried the dress shop owner and, after a quick discussion with her husband, she decided to cancel the building contract for the planned extensions to the dress shop. She rang the builder to pass on the bad news who immediately decided to cancel all the jobs he had planned for the next year. His first call was to the young architect, who started all this off, to tell him his services were no longer required because "a depression is coming".

Bitterly disappointed the young man slunk back to the restaurant to drown his sorrows. This time he was in no hurry and picked up the paper that was still lying there. To his amazement he discovered it was an old paper dated 20 years ago and had been left there by a previous customer who had found it when he was cleaning out some old boxes. The "depression" had all been in the young man's mind but its effects were still as real as if the paper had been printed today.

This story displays the power of negative thinking and should alert you to the importance of keeping a positive attitude. How do you become a positive person? The best way is to make it a habit but like all other habits it needs to be practised until it is firmly in place.

You will find that life seems to work in circles that go round and round to lift you up, or round and round to pull you down. Negative thinkers fear the worst and therefore subconsciously probably don't try as hard. It usually takes time and effort to produce a worthwhile result and there are often set-backs along the way. How could you possibly stick with a project if you believed you would fail.

There is more to PMA than the value of ongoing motivation that it provides. You should also be aware of the principle of positive and negative attraction as espoused by Napoleon Hill. His theory is that electrical waves in the brain attract to you what you fear or truly desire. Because negative thinkers put out negative vibrations they find that the outcomes they fear come true exactly as they predicted. Consequently their belief that they are always "cursed" by bad luck is reinforced. They are on a downhill path.

In *Pathfinders* Gail Sheehy writes "a person with a positive outlook is more likely to attract friendship and love which promise in turn the richer intimacy and emotional supports that characterise overall life satisfaction . . . people who allow themselves to become soured on life often set in motion a self-reinforcing cycle. Their anger or self-pity becomes so off-putting that it deprives them of the friends and help they otherwise would deserve."[2]

Now think about those who have read what is in this book and are starting to put it into practice. They have set practical goals, they are discovering how to make them happen and they are working hard to develop their skills which is building their self esteem. They don't worry about following the crowd because they understand that "most people" are going in the wrong direction. They are not concerned about making mistakes because they know that failure is at worst an opportunity to learn. They can therefore face the future with confidence.

Watch how it all works together. Their brains are putting out the right "vibes", they are being noticed because of the extra effort they are putting in, and life is steadily improving for them. As their lives start to get better they create a success pattern for themselves on which they can build. Their positive mental attitudes have helped them to do all this but, in turn, the results of their positive thinking encourage them to maintain a positive attitude.

---

2. Sheehy, Gail. *Pathfinders* 1981:21 Bantam

14

GIVE IT A TRY

You cannot teach a man anything. You can only help him discover it within himself.

Galileo

The message in this chapter is that you should try to have as many learning experiences as possible. You may have heard the saying "luck is what happens when preparedness meets opportunity" therefore it should follow that the better and wider the preparation the more chance there is for opportunity to pop up with "luck" to follow.

Have you ever gone to the beach on a summer's day when the weather is slightly cool despite the season? The ocean looks wonderful and you walk across the sand and try the water with your toe. Feels icy. You go through the same old pattern of "Let's go in" "No, it's too cold" "Well, maybe". Then the sheer joy of the day overcomes you and you take the plunge. The first reaction might be a scream as the water hits your back but in less than 30 seconds you are bobbing along happily saying "It's not too bad, after all".

Most of life's situations are like that. You face a barrier and are initially put off by the apparent difficulty of it. However you finally find the courage to cross it and then almost always discover it wasn't nearly as hard as you thought it was going to be. These barriers are important points in your life and you will keep striking them as long as you continue growing. They are important because your reaction when you meet each one affects the way you face other barriers.

If you stop and refuse to take the plunge you are reinforcing behaviour that will probably happen again at the next barrier. You will find it harder and harder to make progress. On the other hand if you **do** act, the next

THE SPECTATOR...

TANDBERG

barrier will be easier to attack because you are forming habits that will help you make progress. As the great doctor and writer Maxwell Maltz said *Close scrutiny will show that most . . . 'crisis situations' are . . . opportunities to either advance or stay where we are.*

In 1991 the grazier Sara Henderson was named Australian Businesswoman of the Year. Her autobiography is an inspiring read and gives a graphic account of the hardships she faced throughout her life. These include a severe car smash when she was 16, almost dying while giving birth to a child, being trapped in a raging typhoon near Hong Kong, and facing bankruptcy when her husband died leaving her with a huge string of debts. She writes "The knowledge you gain from your experiences, good or bad, would not have been gained if you had not had the experiences! You must experience to grow, with growth comes knowledge and with knowledge you change·"[1]

I now spend much of my time doing radio work and making speeches to large audiences. Let me assure you I wasn't born with a talent for that; in fact I once had a speech impediment that made my early years a misery. My speaking career started at age 21 when my employer, the Bank, offered to pay for any staff who wished to improve their public speaking skills by joining Rostrum – a public speaking club. As far as I know I was the **only** person who took up the offer. Everybody else was too scared of speaking in public. Naturally I was as frightened as the rest of them but I was prepared to make the effort to learn this valuable skill.

Going to Rostrum was a terrifying experience at first and I had a particular problem in that my knees used to shake violently whenever I got up to speak. If you rub a stick along a dog's back and watch how the legs twitch you will get the picture. It was hard going at first but as I persevered it got easier, and after a few months of embarrassment even my knees stopped knocking.

Time passed and through hard work and study I found myself working in the Bank's International Division dealing with foreign currencies. The Bank asked for a volunteer to give a monthly lecture on foreign currency at the staff training school. As usual I was the only volunteer but I saw it as a further chance to develop my speaking skills and to "pose" as a VIP once a month by being driven to the school in a large, black, chauffeur-driven car.

Later, when I was running a building and real estate

---

1. Henderson Sara. *From Strength to Strength* 1990:304 Macmillan.

company, the Real Estate Institute offered six people (including me) the chance to go to Canberra for a two day weekend course on public speaking run by the renowned speaker Doug Malouf. Three refused but the rest of us saw it as a further chance for skill development. The course was even better than we had hoped and we all benefited greatly from it.

Learning is an exciting process because the moment you acquire a new skill, or a piece of knowledge, a chance comes up to put it into use.

Just three days after I returned from the course the ABC rang to ask if I would do a talkback radio session for three Tuesday nights between 10 pm and midnight. Naturally I agreed and, using the knowledge I had gained at the Doug Malouf course, managed to convince the local Sunday paper to do a feature story promoting the program. I had pulled the double, the ABC and the paper were both promoting the segment. Thus the program received maximum publicity and the phone lines ran hot.

While all this was going on I also made the time to sharpen up my writing skills by putting a weekly 400 word column in the local paper. This forced me to find a topical subject each week, write about it in an interesting way and to meet deadlines. All very useful skills.

A few weeks later another local station 4BC rang me to see if I would like to host a real estate and finance program between 6 and 7 on Saturday mornings. Once again I accepted the offer but figured that **nobody** would have the slightest interest in finance at that hour. I was wrong, many people who are interested in finance are early risers and many others forget to turn their clock radios off on Friday nights. In any event I developed a loyal bunch of listeners as I further honed up on my talkback radio skills. What was more important was that I was being kept in touch with what the public needed to know.

Time passed and eventually I started writing a weekly finance column in the Brisbane *Courier Mail*. One fateful morning a woman rang the radio program to tell me she liked what I was saying and asked me to name some books in which she could read more about the topics I spoke about and wrote about. I promised her I would check out the bookstores during the week and tell her and all the other listeners next Saturday morning.

What do you think I discovered? There was nothing in the book shops that covered finance in a simple way. Sure there were American books showing you how to turn $1 into a million quickly and easily (!!!) and thick academic books with tiny print and loads of meaningless graphs that looked too boring to open. However there was nothing that covered the vital subject of finance in a way that enabled the average reader to benefit from it. I decided to write *Making Money Made Simple*, the book which became an international best-seller and changed the lives of many who read it.

This may have been a long story but sometimes, when I am about to give a speech to a huge audience, or get ready for a radio or television programme, I wonder where I would be today if I had not accepted the Bank's offer and volunteered to join that public speaking club many years ago.

Most people will never get out of their comfort level and try something new, yet it is only by trying new experiences that we can reach our full potential. It doesn't matter if the experience is helping behind a shop counter, changing a tyre, selling raffle tickets, trying 10 pin bowling or experimenting in the kitchen. Somewhere, someday it will be useful to you even if it shows you what you don't want to do. My wife and I love to run the Devonshire Tea stall at the school fete because just one day a year of standing on our feet working so hard gets rid of any urges we might have to own a restaurant.

Ann Lewin was a a young woman when we met about 20 years ago. She had a small shop "Lady Leather" in Fortitude Valley in Brisbane where she made leather hats and belts. The shop grew and she expanded her range by making other leather goods. She changed course and started selling real estate but soon found that was not to her liking and started designing and making elegant lingerie. She has done so well that the Ann Lewin name is now known world-wide and Ann lives in New York running the fashion empire she has created. It all happened because Ann has never been afraid to "give it a try".

I'll bet when you were a child you weren't frightened to give it a try. If you were like all the children I know you were into everything; eating dirt, running naked on the beach in winter, poking your fingers into the dog's mouth, talking to strangers.

Now you're probably different. Now you know about fear and embarrassment and rejection and peer pressure and that dare-devil try anything attitude has been replaced by a feeling of "What will happen if I try this and it hurts, or it doesn't work, or I end up feeling silly?"

If you feel like that when you face a new situation ask yourself "What is the worst thing than can happen if this goes wrong?". Most likely you will find at worst it may be a bit of temporary embarrassment.

The following may touch a chord with you:

> *To laugh is to risk appearing a fool, to weep is to risk appearing sentimental.*
>
> *To reach out to another is to risk involvement, to expose feelings is to risk exposing your true self.*
>
> *To place your ideas and dreams before a crowd is to risk their loss.*
>
> *To love is to risk not being loved in return, to live is to risk dying,*
>
> *To hope is to risk despair, to try is to risk failure.*
>
> *But risks must be taken because the greatest hazard in life is to risk nothing.*
>
> *The person who risks nothing, does nothing, has nothing, is nothing.*
>
> *He may avoid suffering and sorrow, but he cannot learn, feel, change, grow or live.*
>
> *Chained by his certitudes he is a slave that has forfeited all freedom. Only a person who risks is free.*

Anon

15

UNIVERSAL LAWS

The gifts that one receives for giving are so immeasurable
that it is almost an injustice to accept them.

Rod McKuen

This chapter will explain two fundamental laws that are understood and followed by truly successful people. They remind me of the concept of love, difficult to define and measure, but still very much in existence. You may question what follows or it may confirm what you believe but in any event it will pay to know about these laws. You may pay a heavy price if you break them.

THE LAW OF GIVING AND RECEIVING

Let's talk first about the law of giving and receiving. It has been put in many forms. My father always told me "If you do a good turn you'll get two good turns back". My primary school teacher taught us the Golden Rule "Do unto others as you would have them do unto you". The Chinese philosopher Lao-Tzu said "He who obtains has little. He who scatters has much". I hear many people say now "What goes around comes back". The meaning remains the same no matter how you say it.

Most of my friends and I believe in what we call the great "bank in the sky". You do good turns whenever you have the opportunity and think of them as placing deposits of good turns in some mythical bank. Then when the time comes, as it always does, that you need a good turn or a helping hand you will find that somebody will be waiting to help you. Usually the good turns don't come from the same people you have helped but they certainly come back. Sure, I know it sounds weird but it works for my friends and for my family.

As your awareness grows and you read more books on success you will notice the concept cropping up continually. In his audio program *"Transformation – You'll See It When You Believe It"* psychologist Dr Wayne Dyer tells about the mechanic who came to his beach house to fix up the refrigerator. The mechanic was loaded down with problems which he talked about at great length. After an hour had passed Dr Dyer had given him a complete counselling session as well as numerous books and tapes free. The mechanic was amazed that anybody could be so generous and exclaimed "Mister, how come you can give so much away without going broke?" Dyer smiled as he replied "When you know the answer, you won't have to ask the question". You see he knew about the law of giving and receiving – the more you give away the more you get back.

In *Law of Success* Napoleon Hill points out that the Golden Rule is based on the principle of sowing and reaping which ensures that you will reap more than you sow both positive and negative. If this is so obvious why do so many people fail to practise it. Probably because there are two types of people – those who focus on scarcity and those who focus on abundance.

The ones who focus on scarcity see the world as a dangerous jungle. They work on the principle that everything is in short supply and only those who jump in quickly and knock everybody aside will survive. They spend their lives in constant fear. Fear they won't have enough to live on, fear somebody else will beat them to a promotion, fear they will get sick. You can recognize them because their lives are in such conflict that they seldom achieve any sort of happiness.

I met a person with a severe case of scarcity thinking

when I was giving a speech in Fiji. Contrary to popular perception it's often lonely when you are far from home in some other country and I had been trying to find a golf partner to fill in an afternoon. A widow from Chicago decided to join me and we set off for the golf course that was nearly 30 kilometres from the hotel. She spent the entire journey to the course worrying if there would be a time to play available for us. When we got there she was worried that it might rain. During the round she worried all the time that she would lose her ball and as we neared the final hole she expressed concern that we might not find a taxi to take us home.

On the way home she worried we might be late for dinner and during dinner she did not have a glass of wine in case she got too drunk to pack. She will never re-marry lest the new husband dies like the first one did, and she won't go out with men in case she gets hurt in a relationship. When I left her she was concerned that all her clothes would not fit in her suitcase!

The opposites are people who focus on abundance. They have acquired a positive mental attitude which helps them reframe a bad situation, they understand that failure is no more than a learning experience and they believe that somehow things will work out for the best. Because they feel this way they are usually optimistic, happy people who are always ready to share with others.

As you delve further into this subject you will find that many writers believe we attract into our lives what we focus on, or what we think we are.

Those who focus on abundance attract prosperity; those who focus on lack attract all the negative things. Notice how this goes round and round. Because the prosperity thinkers have an optimistic view of the world they automatically practise the law of giving and therefore are assured of receiving.

One of the most famous essays in success literature is *"Compensation"* by the American writer Ralph Waldo Emerson. Napoleon Hill calls it "a must for people who want to understand themselves, understand the world and find wonderful peace of mind that will stay with them".[1]

Emerson writes "Men suffer all their life long under the foolish superstition that they can be cheated. But it is as impossible for a man to be cheated by anyone but himself, as for a thing to be and not to be at the same time".[2]

You can call it what you will; the Golden Rule, the Law of Sowing and Reaping or the Law of Compensation. By any name it means that we finally get back more than we put in. That's what Emerson meant when he said we can only cheat ourselves. By being too lazy or too indifferent to sow, we forfeit the great harvest we could have reaped.

THE LAW OF OPPOSITES

I call this one the law of opposites. That simply means you often have to do the opposite of what seems logical to get the result you want. Here are some examples:

• The more a farmer takes from the land the less it returns in the long term. The way to get the most out is to put the most into it.

• In golf you make the ball rise by hitting down on it. You make it go faster by slowing down your hand action.

• The way to be lovable is to be loving. A person who is frantically trying to make somebody else love them is a sorry sight. It's like the child belting the kitten to make it purr.

• The harder we try to think, the less chance we have of coming up with the right answer. It will come when our minds are relaxed. You must have gone through the experience of having something you were trying to remember on the tip of your tongue and trying harder and harder to remember it without success.

1. Hill Napoleon. *Grow Rich with Peace of Mind*. 1967. 36th printing 1991:139 Fawcett Crest, New York
2. Emerson's Essays 1951:86 Thomas Y Crowell Company New York

Kahlil Gibran wrote "I have learned silence from the talkative, toleration from the intolerant, and kindness from the unkind"[3]. Emerson said "The only reward of virtue is virtue, the only way to have a friend is to be one"[4].

At Bert Weir's Centre Within course[5] I learned the best way to handle feeling unhappy was to find somebody to help, and the best way to boost my own self esteem was to try to make somebody else feel good about themself. That is probably why the happiest people I know are those who spend time helping others.

In the section about successful negotiation in *More Money with Noel Whittaker* I point out the secret of finding the best outcome is to look for a "win/win" situation where both parties get what they want. Let's look at a practical example of this in the light of what we now know about the law of opposites.

You want to borrow the family car to visit your friends, Dad wants it to take to golf. If you both focus only on what you want the outcome is doomed to failure. A bitter argument is almost certain to occur with Dad driving off to golf in a most unhappy state of mind leaving you without wheels. You will probably be miserable for the rest of the day and Dad will most likely play a dreadful round of golf and come home in a worse mood than when he left. You may then regard him as a cruel thoughtless parent and he may regard you as a problem child.

Imagine what would happen if **your** thoughts were focused on making sure Dad got to golf safely and in a happy frame of mind and **his** thoughts were focused on ensuring you had a great day out with your friends. After

---

3. Reported in *Bits & Pieces* (The Economics Press, Fairfield New Jersey) September 17, 1992:12.
4. Essays 1841. Friendship. R.W. Emerson
5. Bert Weir conducts courses at the Relaxation Centre, Brisbane. You can find much of his material in his book *You were Born Special, Beautiful and Wonderful, What Happened* published by the author

a friendly talk during which you both worked out ways to help the other gain what they wanted you might agree that you could drop Dad at the golf course on the way to your friends' place and one of his golfing partners could give him a lift home. Everybody is happy, the outcome is satisfactory for both and the relationship is strengthened. Obviously this has huge benefits for both of you and it all happens because you choose to focus out and not in.

The two laws in this chapter are a part of all religious beliefs and have been known to the human race for centuries. They are as valid now as they have always been and you will notice them occurring everywhere as your awareness develops. Your happiness will grow as you start to work with them.

16

IT'S UP TO YOU

You need only choose . . . then keep choosing as many times as necessary. That is all you need to do. And it is certainly something you can do. Then as you continue to choose, everything is yours.

Vernon Howard

This chapter could also be called "Facing Reality". Its message is that your life is very much in your hands.

That's a harsh way to start, but you must understand it if you are going to make something of your life. Read the quote at the top of this chapter again and think about it. You are where you are now because of the choices you have made to date – the smart choices and the thoughtless choices that all of us make. We are all human and have all done many positive and negative things. However that is in the past. Where you will be in the future depends on the choices you make from now on.

When children are learning to ride a bike they usually suffer many hours of wobbling about, falling over and getting up again. Finally something clicks, it all comes together, and they have no trouble riding a bike again. Learning to take charge of your life is like that. If you continue along the path of self-development a moment will come when you understand that you are in charge of your life. **Once it clicks you will never be the same again.**

Wouldn't life be scary if you weren't in control – if life

was a lottery, and you had no influence over the outcome? It would be like speeding along a busy road in a car with no brakes. Fortunately it's not like that. You **do** have brakes but the road of life has hundreds of intersections and each time you come to one you have to pick which turn to make. If you keep choosing the wrong turn you end up on bad roads. Once you find yourself in the area where all the bad roads are the situation worsens. Finally the only choice you have is between a bad road and a worse road.

To illustrate that point let's think about somebody whom we'll call Tommy who went to an overcrowded school. He could choose between paying attention in class and doing his homework or ignoring both the teacher and the homework. He chose the lazy way and his work got behind that of his class mates. When his problems were discovered he had a choice of going to extra classes to catch up but chose to watch TV instead. He finally dropped out of school.

He then had the option of taking a training program but chose to stay home. He could not get a job, got in with a bad crowd and was enticed to "borrow" a car for a joyride. He ended up in Court. He was let out on probation but chose to break it. Eventually he was sent to jail where the only choices left to him were serving out his time or trying to escape.

Mary got her first job at 19 and had a choice of saving some money and spending what was left, or spending all of her pay and booking up clothes on credit cards. She chose to borrow to buy the extra gear and then faced a choice of buying no more until the debt was paid off or increasing her borrowings. She chose to increase the debt, after all the repayments on $2 000 are only $25 a week, and kept spending as if there was no tomorrow. She was $4 000 in debt after 18 months. Her friends had been saving up to go on an overseas holiday and asked Mary to go with them. Because she had no savings she chose to borrow another $5 000 on a personal loan.

When she came home she became suddenly scared

about how much debt she had. Her friends urged her to seek financial counselling but she chose not to. Finally the strain became too much for her and she lost her job.

Notice that both Tommy and Mary had plenty of chances to take the best road. However each time they decided on a course of action it led to a worse road with less attractive choices. As they made more and more wrong choices the roads got worse and so did the options available to them.

Mary and Tommy are made-up characters to illustrate a point but they are typical of many young people who get into trouble slowly. The sad part is that most of those who do keep making unfortunate choices refuse to take any personal responsibility at all. They blame the "system", "other people" or might shrug it off with "That's just my luck". As you can see luck had very little to do with it.

Notice I said "very little" to do with it because luck **did** play a part. Neither Mary nor Tommy had anybody to teach them they were responsible for their lives or to explain the dangers of getting into debt or being influenced by bad company.

As Brian Tracy pointed out in his audio cassette program *"The Psychology of Success"* the difference between winners and losers is that the losers believe that anything good that happens to them is a lucky break and blame everything bad that happens on somebody or something else. As a result they never take responsibility for what happens in their lives and forever deny themselves the chance to learn.

In contrast the winners take full credit for their successes and treat their failures as a learning experience.

The above is probably obvious when you think about it. If so why do so many people fail to take control of their lives? I believe there are four reasons:

(1) They don't believe they have the ability.

(2) They don't want to put in the effort.

(3) They have been conditioned to believe they are victims.

(4) They don't know how to get started.

We'll now think about each of these in turn and discuss ways to overcome them in the light of what we have read so far.

NO FAITH IN YOUR ABILITY

This is caused by a faulty self-concept which is probably the result of a previous failure pattern created by past failures in your life or because you have always been too frightened to try anything. It can also be caused by your comparing yourself to others in an unfavourable light. You may have noticed that people tend to compare their worst feature to a world figure's best feature. For example they compare their looks to a film star's looks and their sporting skills to that of an international champion.

A good way to start is to stop comparing yourself with others. Then concentrate on becoming an authority on something.

The range of subjects is limitless as the sole aim of the exercise is for you to prove to yourself you have the ability to do it. It could be skating, knowing the history of the local football team, rock music, cooking pikelets, growing roses, making model aeroplanes, or, if you are a junior in an office, knowing how to save postage. That last one might not sound too exciting but the postage rates are confusing and nothing will get you noticed quicker than coming up with ways to save your boss money.

Once you become an "expert" in your chosen subject, and also practise the techniques described in the chapter on self-concept, you will find your faith in yourself will grow as you start to enjoy a small measure of self esteem.

NOT WANTING TO PUT IN THE EFFORT

Often it has been said that winners are those who do what losers are unwilling to do and the cold reality is that making the effort is one of the factors that sets the winners apart. By now you should be aware that everything has a price but finally the rewards that come from that price far outweigh it. Remember Emerson's Law of Compensation I mentioned on page 89.

From my observations it is lack of motivation, not laziness, that afflicts so many. Why do some people who have to drag themselves to work for five days of the week leap out of bed at 4 am to go fishing on Sunday morning? Where does the energy come from to party all night?

The way to overcome the lack of enthusiasm for work is to find a job you enjoy, because when you have done that you have turned your work into a hobby. The best way to do this is to keep learning and finding new experiences to try until you find your niche. I found I had triple the energy when I started my own business for, at last, the responsibilities and the rewards were mine.

BAD CONDITIONING

If you have come from a family background where it is the normal practice to blame everybody else for what goes wrong you will have to do some quiet thinking. It is unlikely you will change the views of the older members of the family so you will have to compensate for their negative input with positive material from other sources.

Try to find some positive people to mix with and if possible start, or join, a mastermind group. The material listed at the back of this book will help and as you read and understand more, you will see the negative input from those close to you for what it is.

NOT KNOWING HOW TO GET STARTED

Maybe you don't know how to start. Possibly you have so many other things on your plate that you can't make the time to start or perhaps you are just the victim of good old procrastination. Whatever it is you should understand that commencing any project is nearly always difficult. The hardest part of writing a book is preparing the chapter outlines; my friend Rick Everingham the painter tells me that nothing is more difficult than staring at a blank canvas. The great Russian author Fyodor Dostoevsky said *Taking a new step, uttering a new word, is what people fear most.* The Scottish writer Samuel Smiles believed *The reason why so little is done is generally because so little is attempted.*

You start by setting practical and simple goals. Then you use the "Salami Technique" which I mentioned in the chapter on Goal Setting to make some steady progress. Once you make that first step the rest will fall into place.

It can be difficult to move out of the comfort zone and start to accept full responsibility for your actions. However only by doing this can you take charge of your life and direct it where you want to go. Your future is safer in your hands than in the hands of somebody else and infinitely more fulfilling.

17

THE REALITY OF MONEY

If you make money your God, it will plague you like the Devil.

Henry Fielding

In this chapter I will explain what money is and what it can, and can't, do for you.

We live in a rich country where opportunities abound and where most people who are young now will earn millions of dollars before they stop work. Yet most of them will spend all their lives worrying about money and retire with nothing more than a house and a few thousand dollars in the bank.

The knowledge you are gaining will enable you to be different and when you have read this book you should be able to work towards a goal of complete financial security if you wish. In the next few chapters I will show you how to make money, how to spend it and how to accumulate it.

Before money was around people used the barter system. You shod my horse and I gave you some eggs and butter in return. That was a cumbersome process and people found that coins were simpler as they solved such obvious problems as trying to barter a bale of hay for half a horse. The wealthier ones hoarded gold which was usually left at the goldsmith's for safe keeping. The goldsmith gave out receipts for each bar of gold and if you needed some gold to pay a debt you went to the goldsmith, handed over your receipt, withdrew the required amount of gold and delivered it to your creditor in payment.

This was also cumbersome and the citizens found it was easier to use the receipts themselves as a means of exchange. If I owed you two bars of gold I simply signed two of my receipts over to you. This entitled you to withdraw two of my bars of gold from the goldsmith when you wished. After a time the receipts themselves started to act as money and eventually few holders bothered to go to the goldsmith to withdraw the physical gold.

As civilisation grew, and business became more complex, banks gradually replaced the goldsmiths and finally receipts issued by banks took over from the goldsmith's receipts. Then the banks started to issue their own "bank notes" (a note is a term for a loan document) because it was more convenient for their customers to have money in various denominations.

However banks are not immune from disaster and occasionally a note issuing bank would go broke causing huge losses to those unfortunate people who held notes issued by it. One by one the government of each country took over the issuing of money and the banks gave up doing it.

As you can see the need for convenience changed the system and it is still changing today. We now live in a society where many people hardly see money at all. Their pay goes direct into their account and they withdraw it by debit card or by writing cheques. Despite the change in the method of completing a transaction the essential nature of money has not changed – it is a means of exchange. It enables us to exchange our goods and services for the goods and services of others.

Unfortunately far too many people focus on accumulating money and forget the main game which is to have a happy and fulfilled life. The Bible says *"For we brought nothing into this world, and it is certain we can carry nothing out . . . The love of money is the root of all evil"*[2]. Money cannot buy happiness, health, fine weather, contentment or good relationships and I doubt if there are many wealthy old people who would not give up all of their wealth in exchange for being young again.

However make no mistake about it – money is important in the areas where it works. These include providing a home, a good education, top health care, the

---

2. 1 Timothy ch. 6

opportunity to help others, clothes and the chance to experience the excitement of travel. What I like about money is that it enables you to make more choices in your life, choices that are based on what you **want** to do, not what you **have** to do.

My wife and I travel a lot and we have eaten occasionally at restaurants that are recognised as the finest in the world. We have done it for the experience but are far happier eating in cheap sidewalk restaurants where the food is a quarter of the price and nobody minds if you strike up a conversation with the people at the next table to practise the language. The point is that having money allows us a genuine choice – we eat at the sidewalk restaurants because we prefer to be there.

Now let's consider a few basics.

MONEY WON'T MAKE YOU HAPPY

Most of us have dreamed of having millions of dollars in a foreign bank and spending life cruising around the world in yachts or going to fancy parties. If that's your goal, and you work hard and give up enough for it, you might even get there. However in reality most of that stuff is dreamed up by Hollywood script writers and, although the fancy mansions and the huge yachts do exist, there is plenty of evidence that the lifestyle does not make for happiness. If you want proof go to the local library and read some biographies about the so called glamorous people.

It came as a shock to me to discover there was almost no connection between money and happiness. The happiest person I know is a 65-year-old woman who rents a small apartment and has less than $5 000 in the bank. She was well off once but a gambling husband lost it all and left her to bring up a large family alone. She has coped magnificently with such a personal tragedy and lives a happy and fulfilled life. In contrast I know wealthy people who are often unhappy because they don't realise that enjoying what they have is more important than the amount of money they have. Above all it is the ability to enjoy life that makes for real happiness.

However there is a huge connection between being unhappy and having money troubles. It is no fun to watch your car being towed away because you failed to make the payments, to arrive home to find your power and phone have been cut off, or to lose your home because of interest rate rises.

WHY ACCUMULATE MONEY?

Money is a medium that enables you to exchange your services for that of another. However by itself it is useless – if you are stranded in a burning hot desert a suitcase full of money won't quench your thirst. What counts is what it can do for you. Having money to spend may make you feel good, it may provide a feeling of freedom or security and for many people it is even a way of keeping score.

Because you use money to pay for another's services, and you receive money by providing services, you should understand how it follows that the amount of money you get depends on how much service you give.

I have stressed it is preferable to have control over your life. Even though money won't make you happy building up a store of investment capital will provide financial security and enable you to have more choices in what you do. Think about the following:

(1) When you have money saved up you can pay cash for what you want instead of borrowing and paying interest. As most people pay hundreds of thousands of dollars in interest over a lifetime it follows that reducing the interest you pay gives you money available for more productive purposes. If Sally is paying $300 a month in car repayments and Anne has a car that is free of debt, Anne has $300 a month more spending money available.

(2) The investment capital you build up provides opportunities for you. It is likely you will have a chance to start your own business at some stage in your life which usually requires you to have some money to put towards

it. Wouldn't it be a shame if you missed an exciting money-making opportunity just because you had neglected to build up some capital for that purpose?

(3) Building up money gives you confidence in your ability to generate income and accumulate wealth. Once you have this confidence you know you can do it and you won't be frightened to invest some of your capital in riskier projects. Fear of loss has held many people back and it is true that as you get older you are less able to take large risks because you do not have the time to rebuild your wealth. If you are going to lose some money it is better to do it when you are young. Wouldn't it be a tragedy to realise when you are old that you could have achieved your dreams but fear of loss held you back and you didn't get around to having a go.

(4) Money gives you more freedom. Once you have established a capital base, either by accumulating income-producing investments or by building up a business, you can take a break from your job to explore other areas in your life. Certainly it takes time to get to that stage but it's a wonderful feeling to be able to take a month off to trek through the mountains or even to take a morning off to attend one of your children's sports days.

Now that you understand what money can, and can't, do for you we'll move to the principles of building wealth.

18

HOW TO BE RICH!!!

*However easy it may be to make money, it is the most
difficult thing in the world to keep it*
P.T. BARNUM

In this chapter I'll teach you how to start to build a
fortune. It is done by the combination of slowly
accumulating capital and letting the magic of compound
interest work on it for you.

You have now read over two-thirds of this book and
your eyes should be starting to open. You know you can
do more than you are presently doing to build on your
potential and that success, whatever it means in your
case, is not a matter of chance. It requires discipline and
work. Now it's time to let you in on the secrets of building
wealth. Like the other principles in this book the secrets of
wealth accumulation are not difficult nor are they hard to
understand – it's purely a matter of getting into the habit
of applying them.

STEP ONE – MANAGE YOUR MONEY

The first key to becoming wealthy is to learn to manage
your money effectively. Tens of thousands of people earn
big money and are always broke because the money just
slips through their fingers. Obviously earning lots of
dollars is meaningless if you spend them all, so any
wealth building plan depends on your grabbing hold of

some of that money as it comes pouring in. Even though it's obvious "most people" don't do it.

There is a simple and effective tool called a budget for managing your money. I'll tell you about it in the next chapter. If you don't have a budget you will have no idea where your money went. Worse still you will end up wasting most of it.

STEP TWO – UNDERSTAND HOW SMALL THINGS ACCUMULATE

People seldom succeed or fail in one great earth shattering event. Rather it is the succession of small things done, or not done, that makes the difference. Mark saves 10% of each pay and Charles spends a little more than he gets each pay by booking up goods on credit cards. That mightn't sound much but after two years Mark has $5 000 in the bank and Charles is $5 000 in debt. They are now $10 000 apart.

Robin spends just an hour a day studying material that will improve her work skills, Kim spends the same hour watching TV. It's only an hour a day but after three years Robin has given over 1 000 hours to study and has become a leader in her field. Kim is now wondering why Robin is now so successful and earning double what she earns.

In 1980 I showed home buyers how they could save thousands of dollars in home interest by making their payments weekly or fortnightly. For example if a couple borrows $60 000 at 12% the repayments over 30 years are $618 a month making a total of $222 480. The principal repaid is $60 000 and total interest is $162 480. Just by changing the repayments to $309 a fortnight the term drops to 19 years and the total repayments fall to $152 760. That's a saving of almost $70 000. Back in 1980 the banks all laughed at the idea but now most of them are advertising it. Better still, most homebuyers are doing it and speeding up their wealth creation process as well.

It seems like witchcraft but it's really simple if you think about it. There are 12 calendar months in a year but 26 fortnights – by making the payments fortnightly you pay back an extra $620 a year without realising it. Because of the magic of compound interest (discussed in a later chapter) this extra $620 a year makes a massive difference.

Now notice one important factor. Most of the borrowers who are using this new system to save tens of thousands of dollars never had a cent to spare when they were paying monthly. Probably they still haven't got a cent to spare. Nevertheless, by changing the payment frequency, they end up paying back an extra $620 a year.

Where did the money to pay that extra $620 a year come from? You will find a detailed answer in the chapter titled "The Secret of Wealth" in *Making Money Made Simple* but it is enough to say here that most of us meet any commitments that we undertake. This is what causes the extraordinary power of goal setting, where many small actions add up to a mighty result.

STEP THREE – KNOW ABOUT THE BOTTOM LINE

The bottom line is an accounting term that refers to a company's profit. In simple terms a profit and loss account looks like this:

Gross Business Income	$500 000
Cost of Running the business	$450 000
Net Profit	$50 000

As you can clearly see the term "bottom line" refers to the net profit because that's where it is placed when the financial statements are drawn up.

Now think about your own little profit and loss account.

Income after tax	$ 20 000
Costs of your lifestyle	$ 19 000
Amount left over for wealth creation	$ 1 000

The term "costs of your lifestyle" includes food, clothes, rent, loan repayments, entertainment, holidays, and fares

– all the items on which most people spend their money. Notice that, while they are expenses you often can't avoid, they are all consumed and have no lasting value. Therefore they are **not** available for creating wealth. You build wealth with the money you have over.

Imagine what would happen if you could increase your net income by 10% without increasing the costs of your lifestyle. Then your personal profit and loss account would read:

Income after tax	$ 22 000
Costs of your lifestyle	$ 19 000
Amount left over for wealth creation	$ 3 000

TANDBERG

You have just increased the amount you have left for wealth creation by 300% by increasing your net income by 10%. Isn't that a perfect example of the law of sowing and reaping; you always reap **much more** than you sow.

Re-read the section above slowly and stop and think about it. **It will change your life forever if you truly**

understand it. I have just taught you one of the most powerful secrets of wealth in the world – increasing your income without increasing your costs.

What would "most people" do? Every time they increase their income they also increase their living costs. As the British humorist Parkinson put it "Expenditure rises to meet income"[1]. Consequently they regard an increase in pay of $2 000 as an excuse to go on a spending spree. It would **never** occur to them that they had just missed the opportunity to **treble** their investment capital. As a result they go through life broke and will continue to blame "the system".

STEP FOUR – MINIMISE BORROWING FOR DEPRECIATING ITEMS

A major difference between financial winners and financial losers is that the winners borrow for items such as houses that gain in value, and the losers borrow for items such as furniture that drop in value. Resist the temptation to start buying goods on credit cards, avoid hire purchase and personal loans and if possible delay buying a car if you have to borrow for it. Use the family car for as long as possible.

This is such an important topic that several chapters in *Making Money Made Simple* are devoted to it.

STEP FIVE – APPRECIATE THE IMPORTANCE OF INCREASING YOUR INCOME STREAM

Think of financial independence as a destination and the assets you accumulate along the way as the vehicle to get you there. The income you earn is the fuel that drives the vehicle – the more you can earn the faster will be the trip **provided** you use the income for wealth creation and not for consumer spending.

1. Parkinson. C.N. *The Law and the Profits* (1960) Chapter 1.

Unfortunately "most people" seem to believe the more you make the more tax you pay and therefore it is not worthwhile making the effort. Probably deep down they are too lazy to stretch themselves to provide the extra service to make the extra money. It's a stupid way to think whatever their reasoning. There are many legal devices that can minimise tax, particularly if you have your own business or have investments.

I've been a high income earner and a low income earner. Take it from me, being a high income earner is best.

STEP SIX – USE YOUR INCOME TO ACQUIRE ASSETS

You now know the importance of putting money aside for wealth creation. It can be done in two ways. By saving the money you have left over after paying your tax and your living expenses, or by using tax effective borrowing.

Tax effective borrowing means borrowing to buy assets that produce income. For example you may buy an investment house for $130 000 with a $100 000 loan. Suppose the rents you receive are $6 000 after you have paid such items as rates, insurance and maintenance. This is taxable income but the interest costs of $11 000 may be taken from your taxable income. The difference of $5 000 between what you received and what you paid out can be claimed as a tax deduction. Consequently the Tax Office is paying part of your interest bill.

THE FORMULA

We call this technique "negative gearing" and full details are given in *Making Money Made Simple*. I recommend it **only** after you have bought the home in which you live and have paid it off. I mention it here to show you why it is so important to increase your income. Then when you have bought and paid off that first home you will have both the asset base and the income stream to speed you along.

As you can see the way to wealth can be summarised as follows:

(1) To build wealth you first have to produce income. You do this by improving your skills.

(2) Don't spend all you earn, keep some to invest.

(3) As your investment capital grows it too will produce income. Now you have two sources of income – from your assets and from your work.

(4) As your assets grow use them, plus the money they are making for you, to buy more income producing assets.

Naturally it takes time, particularly in the early stages, but you will discover in the next chapters that the process gets faster and faster as time goes by. **It will never start unless you earn money and keep some of it to invest.**

19

BUDGETING

*The structure . . . will automatically provide the pattern
for the action which follows.*

Donald Curtis

This chapter will teach you the importance of having a
system to keep your finances on track and to prevent
you frittering your money away.

The early chapters in this book concentrated on helping
you improve the way you manage **yourself** to ensure you
develop your personal potential. The next few chapters
will show you how to manage your **money** so you get the
best out it. There is little doubt you will earn a higher than
average income if you follow the principles in this book
but there is not much to be gained by having a high
income if you waste every cent of it. The solution is to
form the habit of managing your money properly.

First you have to understand a system called a budget.
It's explained in full in *Making Money Made Simple* and
you can study it in detail when you read that book. In this
chapter I'll give you the basics.

THE FIRST PAY CHEQUE

Let's go back to basics and imagine you have found
your first job, are still living at home, and have just
received your first pay packet. Congratulate yourself, you
have taken a vital step to independence by earning some
money of your own. You have just turned on a tap from

which millions of dollars are going to gush in your lifetime. It's like finding an oil well in your back yard that will support you for life. You are now on the road to wealth **provided** you develop a few simple habits.

This may be a fitting time to reflect once more that "most people" never get to learn about these habits, much less practise them. They will also earn millions of dollars in their working life but will be constantly broke and will finish up with their hands stretched out for the welfare cheque. The techniques in this book will give you the opportunity to live differently if you start to practise them.

Because you are young the first pay cheque probably won't be a big one and the natural reaction is to say to yourself "I'll spend all of this but when I start to earn big money I'll put a plan in place to manage my money properly and make it grow." If you start thinking like that you will join "most people" who continually say "If I win the Lotto I'll start to take care of my money." It's an irony because if they had always taken care of their money they wouldn't be worried about winning the Lotto today. They're the same people who say "If I had a good body I'd look after it".

Can you see now how it all works together. Life's losers say they will go the extra mile at work **after** they get the promotion and manage their money properly **after** they become wealthy. Unfortunately for them life doesn't work like that.

It's not the money that counts, it's the habit. Therefore you should look upon that first money you earn as giving you an opportunity to start developing good habits that will give you an edge on everybody else.

The major goal is to get into the habit of living within your means, something "most people" never do. When people spend even just a little more than they earn they have to borrow small amounts to get by. This is called going into debt which can be like contracting a slow creeping disease. It is so important that I have devoted two chapters to it in this book.

Your other goal should be to save a portion of each pay. How much? If you are living at home probably 20% of your net pay is reasonable. It is easier to save a larger part of your income while you are living at home and can get cheap board and perhaps the use of the family car.

Now I know that saving $30 a week out of a wage of $150 will seem like chicken feed and probably after a few weeks you'll look at your bank balance of a couple of hundred dollars and wonder if such small amounts of savings are worth worrying about.

Let's repeat the secret – it's not the money, it's the habit. Most of your peers will save nothing, or worse still, will already be starting to acquire the habit of depending on credit cards. By saving 20% of your take home pay, and living within your means, you will put a habit in place that will virtually guarantee you will be one of the few people who become wealthy.

However, you have to beware of the power of human nature – we tend to spend whatever we get. Ask around and you will find that almost all your friends, and their parents and their friends, have trouble living on their incomes even though they all have different incomes.

The trick is to have the 20% you wish to save deducted from your salary and paid straight to a special account with your bank, building society or credit union. If you do that, and put money away in another account for essential expenses, you can spend the rest on clothes, records and having fun with a clear conscience.

This is also a good time to practise your newly acquired knowledge of setting goals. Why not plan to have a special holiday in 12 months time? Work out the cost of it, open a special holiday account, and put in part of the cost each week. Start that habit now and you are assured of good holidays for the rest of your life.

Now you understand the theory of budgeting let's move to the practical part and prepare one. It is simply a matter of preparing a schedule that lists your income followed by the items on which you wish to spend your money. I have shown a sample budget and you will notice the items are listed in order of priority with savings at the top of the list and all the "fun" things at the bottom.

The "fun" items such as entertainment and travel are at the bottom because at a pinch you can do without them. They are not as important to your future as savings, fares and food. Unfortunately "most people" spend on the fun things first and find there is never anything left over for savings. Then they promise to start "next week" which of course never comes.

SPECIMEN BUDGET	
Income after tax	$150
ESSENTIAL ITEMS	
Savings a/c	$30
Holiday a/c	10
Fares	15
Grooming	5
Board	15
Self Education Exps	5
Total Essential items	$ 70
BALANCE REMAINING FOR	
Clothes	
Records	
Raging	
Movies etc etc etc	$ 80

After just 12 months there will be nearly $2 000 in the investment savings account and $550 in the holiday account when interest is credited. Can you imagine how good it will feel to know you have saved over **two and a half thousand dollars** in your first year of working.

If you understand the power of budgeting you will quickly establish yourself as a person who can manage money and who can set and achieve goals. The result will be more than a future free of financial problems – it will almost surely mean a great sense of well being and self esteem.

20

UNDERSTANDING INTEREST

*Put each coin to labouring that it may reproduce its kind
even as the flocks of the field and help bring to thee
income, a stream of wealth that shall flow constantly into
thy purse.*[1]

George M Clason.

Interest will make you or break you. Therefore if you are
going to get ahead in this world you will need to
understand the concept of interest and use it to build your
wealth. However interest is like fire – a good servant but a
bad master. In this chapter you will learn how to make it
work to your advantage and how to keep away from the
dangers.

A good way to define interest is "the price paid by
somebody who borrows money to somebody who lends
it".

There are three areas in which people invest the bulk of
their money. In each case the investment gives the person
with the money a benefit. The three areas are:

(1) Money lent out to institutions such as banks, finance
companies, building societies and credit unions who in
turn lend it to people who wish to borrow money. The
borrowers pay interest in return for the use of the money.

---

1. Clason, George *The Richest Man in Babylon* 1985 : 33 Bantam.

(2) Real estate that gives you free shelter if it is your own home or provides you with income in the way of rent if you are a landlord.

(3) Shares in companies. The shares usually provide the investor with a share of the profits in the company by paying profits out as "dividends'.

As you can see if you have money to invest it can be made to give you benefits. These benefits may be more income through interest, rent and dividends; or in the form of free accommodation if you buy a house. However, if you are **receiving** money, there must be somebody **else paying** it out. Obviously it makes sense to be getting it in rather than paying it out. To help you understand this we'll follow a money trail to show you how it all comes together.

HOW TO MAKE INTEREST WORK FOR YOU

Ted and Alice are retired and have over $100 000 in cash. They "deposit" the money in an account at the XYZ Bank and receive interest at the rate of 7% per annum. This means that every year the bank pays them $7 000 for the use of their money.

Bob and Maree are a young couple who have always wanted a home of their own. They have been saving as fast as they can for this home and have accumulated $32 000 in the XYZ Bank. It is paying them 7% interest as well. There's a problem. They have discovered the amount they can save, even with the benefit of the interest the bank is paying them, is not increasing as quickly as the growth in house prices. The only way they can solve the problem is to use somebody else's money to help them buy the house.

The house they want is now selling for $130 000. After some serious discussion they decide to take the plunge and borrow $100 000 from the bank to use to buy the house. They pay the bank 11% for the use of the money although you could say they are using Ted and Alice's money and the bank is acting as the go-between.

Everybody is doing well out of the deal. The retired couple are gaining interest for allowing somebody else to use their money and the young couple now have a house even if it does have a big mortgage. The bank is doing well too – it is paying Ted and Alice $7 000 for the use of the money and collecting $11 000 from Bob and Maree. The profit of $4 000 is used to pay the costs of running the bank, such as staff wages and rent, and the balance is paid to the bank's shareholders as dividends.

You can see now the concept of interest has enabled Ted and Alice to earn money to live on in retirement and it has also helped Bob and Maree to buy a house. It's a win/win situation.

Notice another important point. The only reason Bob and Maree borrowed the money was to enable them to buy the house today instead of waiting to a date in the future when it may cost more. The interest they pay is the price of doing this but **how large** a price is now up to them. It is not like buying a Big Mac where you know the price when you walk into McDonald's. They will continue to pay interest to the bank until the entire loan is paid back.

A SMART WAY TO INVEST MONEY

If they choose to pay it back over a long term, say 30 years, they will have to repay $952 a month. Because of the long term of the loan the repayments in the early years are mainly interest. In fact in the first month the bank keeps $912 of that $952 payment for interest which leaves only $40 a month for reducing the loan balance. Even after five years the bank is taking $892 interest from each monthly payment and a mere $60 is coming off the loan balance.

If they had kept repaying $952 a month for 30 long years Bob and Maree would have paid back $243 000 interest as well as the original sum of $100 000 – a total of $343 000.

The price of borrowing the money to enable them to buy that house today has been nearly a quarter of a million dollars. That's huge!!

There is more bad news. As you learn more about investment you will discover that interest paid on a loan for your own home is not allowed as a tax deduction. Therefore you make your housing repayments from that part of your income that is left after tax has come out. These remaining dollars are called "after tax dollars". Bob and Maree would have to earn over $400 000 just to produce the after tax dollars to pay that interest bill of $243 000.

Luckily Bob and Maree are educated borrowers. They had read my books, were aware of the way interest worked, and had decided to take control of the situation by using all their efforts to pay off the loan quickly. They both worked and repayments of $2 174 a month (that's $281 a week more than they had to pay for the 30 year term) were within their capacity. That extra payment of $281 a week requires total additional repayments of almost $73 000 over the first five years of the loan but after those five years of struggle the loan is repaid. They are free of debt and have a rent free home for life.

Because they invested an extra $73 000 into their mortgage for the first five years they paid only $30 500 in interest as well as the $100 000 principal. The extra payments saved them $212 000 of after tax dollars in interest. That's the equivalent of their earning an extra $400 000 of pre tax dollars!!! Can you think of an easier way to earn $400 000?

There is another benefit. Having the house paid off takes the pressure off the budget if they want to start a family and have to live on one income.

A SILLY WAY TO SPEND INTEREST

Bob and Maree saved thousands of dollars in interest because they were smart enough to invest in an asset that will grow in value and because they knew how much they could save by paying their loan back quickly.

Tom and Kate took a different approach. They decided to buy a car. They had never been savers so took out a loan of $30 000 to cover the entire purchase price. They decided to go for the longest term to keep the repayments down to a level that would allow them plenty of money left over to spend on clothes, nights out and travel. They let the car dealer arrange the finance and found themselves borrowing $30 000 over five years at 17%. The monthly repayment came to $750 and they paid back a total of $44 700 over the five years. The interest bill alone amounted to $14 700, much of which could have been avoided if they had saved a large deposit and paid the loan back over a shorter term.

HOW DELAY AFFECTS INTEREST

If you are a borrower the three factors that influence the total interest you pay are the amount borrowed, the interest rate and the amount you repay each year. You will learn in the next chapter on compound interest about the importance of starting early but you should also understand that a few years delay in buying an item that is growing in value could cost you dearly.

EXAMPLE: *When she was 25 Helen bought a home for $95,000 with $30,000 deposit. She borrowed $65,000 and paid it back over 10 years at $1,000 a month. By her 35th birthday the house was paid off. Her total repayments (principal and interest) were $120,000.*

Peter waited till he was 30 and then paid $150,000 for a similar house because prices had risen. He also put down $30,000 deposit but had to repay $1,400 a month because he borrowed $120 000. The term of the loan was 30 years and his total repayments were over half a million dollars.

Contrast where Helen and Peter will be at age 60 if Helen starts to invest $1 400 a month – the same amount that Peter is paying off his house- from when she is 35. At age 60 Helen may *have accumulated three million dollars, Peter will be making his final house payment.*

WHAT INTEREST DOES

Interest is the price you pay to get some money to use today if you are short of money. The question to ask yourself is "Is it worth paying a price to have spending power available now?" Only you can answer that question but you will find most people borrow money for one of four reasons.

(1) They want to buy an expensive asset such as a house and believe it is better to buy now before prices go up.

(2) They need the use of a depreciating asset such as a washing machine, furniture or a car now and don't have the money available.

(3) They want to indulge themselves with a holiday or to have fun over Christmas but have no available savings.

(4) They have pressing expenses such as the electricity bill to pay but have no money put aside because they haven't managed their money properly. They will suffer unpleasant consequences if the money is not found somehow.

As these topics are covered in detail in *Making Money Made Simple* I will not explore them in detail here. Notice you could argue a case that it is acceptable to borrow for the first two reasons. However if anybody has to borrow for the last two reasons it is obvious they are not practising budgeting or that they suffer from a lack of control.

HOW INTEREST CAN HELP YOU

Once you have money saved up you can invest it and receive interest on it. This means you have increased your income because you now have interest coming in as well as the other income from your work. In the next chapter you will see how the miracle of compound interest can make your savings grow at a faster and faster rate.

If you have to spend money on interest one of the best ways to become wealthy is to buy real estate. Probably the real estate you know best is the house or unit in which you live. If your parents have been following my advice about paying off the loan on the property quickly they may now own the property without any mortgage. Think of the benefits of that. No loan repayments to make, no rent to pay and no fear of being kicked out in the street if the landlord decides to sell the property. That's what I call a feeling of security.

However, even if they own the house now with no mortgage, it is highly likely they borrowed money when they bought it originally. They may have been paying rent of $100 a week and discovered this was nearly as much as the repayments on a home. They decided to buy a place of their own instead of being at the mercy of landlords for the rest of their life. They had to make an important decision. Do they keep on paying rent and try to save the full price of a house, or do they use the money they have as part payment for the house and borrow money for the balance? Luckily for you they took the plunge and bought the house.

You should now appreciate that interest is the price you pay to spend money you don't have. Once you start to borrow you are promising to pay a part of your future income to another person who is the source of the money that has been lent to you. Whether the price is justified is a matter only you can decide.

RENTING...

Owning is better than renting

21

COMPOUND INTEREST

Do not despise the bottom rungs in the ascent to greatness.

Publilius Syrus

Get ready – in this chapter you will have a mathematics lesson. Don't be scared off by the topic because it may well be the most profitable maths lesson you have ever had.

Financial text books often refer to the "magic" of compound interest because what happens when you use it appears to be truly miraculous. You read in a previous chapter that interest is a fee that is paid **to** you for the hire of your money and paid **by** you when you want to hire somebody else's money. The interest is usually paid by the borrower to the lender on a regular basis. Generally this is monthly but it may be quarterly or even yearly.

However there is another way for a lender to receive interest – it may be added to the principal (the amount already owing) and left to grow. This is called compounding the interest because the principal is then bigger as a result of the compounded interest. Notice how when this happens the borrower is paying interest on interest. This interest on the interest may also be compounded and when the next lot of interest is due it is also added to the principal and the compounded interest. Now the poor borrower is paying interest on interest on interest.

This is how it works:

Loan $10 000. Interest Rate 10%. Interest is due each year and is compounded by being added to the principal.

Year One

Original sum borrowed	$10 000
Interest for first year	1 000
Balance owing end of Year One	$11 000

Year Two

Opening balance	$11 000
Interest for second year	1 100
Balance end of Year Two	$12 100

Year Three

Opening balance	$12 100
Interest for third year	1 210
Balance end of Year Three	$13 310

That all looks innocent doesn't it? It may until you analyse the figures. After just three years the borrowers owe 32% more than they originally borrowed. Moreover the interest bill in the third year is 21% more than the interest for the first year. It's often been called creeping into big trouble.

You can work out the effect of compound interest by using the Rule of 72[1]. Write down the number 72 and divide it by the interest rate. The answer is the number of years for the amount you owe to double. If we use 10% from the example above it looks like:

$$\frac{72}{10\%} = 7.2 \text{ years.}$$

Using the Rule of 72 we have now calculated that $10 000 would double in just over seven years if the interest was allowed to compound instead of being paid to the lender at regular intervals. Therefore after 7.2 years the

---

1. Full details of the Rule of 72 are in *Making Money Made Simple*.

borrowers would owe $20 000 instead of the $10 000 they borrowed at the start.

Let's go a step further and imagine we left the money untouched for another seven years. The debt would double again. Now the hapless borrowers would owe $40 000. That's right – in just 14 years because of compound interest the borrowers would owe **four times** what they borrowed in the first place. Leave this compounding process for another seven years and the debt is $80 000.

Think about that for a minute. The $10 000 has grown to $80 000 in just 21 years. It has increased by 800%. That's an average of 38% each year on the original sum.

Notice how compounding starts slowly and gets faster and faster and faster. It is just like an avalanche that may start with a few stones sliding down a mountain and picks up speed and size as the stones collect rocks. These rocks in turn collect huge boulders until the avalanche is like a torrent of stone pounding down the slope.

"How does this affect me?" you may be thinking. It affects you in two ways depending on whether you are a borrower or a lender. Once you understand the principles of compound interest you can avoid being trapped into dangerous levels of debt by compound interest and you can also use the knowledge to slowly build a fortune. This is because it can speed up the rate at which your money grows. For example in the chapter about baby James and the Magic Train in *More Money with Noel Whittaker* I tell how an investment of $2.73 a day could grow at such at rate that when James has his 21st birthday he is receiving almost $52 a day in interest on his $2.73 a day investment.

The problem for "most people" who try to build wealth through compounding is that the compounding process starts slowly and they tire of it before it has had a chance to work. Then they cash in the investment and blow the money on a trip or a car.

The following example will show you how your money can grow. Imagine you put $10 000 into an investment that paid you a return of 12% compounded. The end of year values would be:

End of Year 1	11 200
End of Year 5	17 620
End of Year 10	31 060
End of Year 15	54 730
End of Year 20	96 460
End of Year 25	170 000
End of Year 30	299 580
End of Year 35	527 960
End of Year 40	930 440

Notice how the growth for the first five years is only $7 720, in the second five years $13 440 yet in the last five years $402 480. There is almost as much growth in those last five years as there was in the first 35 years.

This is why it is so important to start building your wealth at a young age.

In the example above there is interest of only $7 620 in those first five years and you could rightly claim it's insignificant. However a 35-year program would return $527 960 and a 40-year program would return $930 440. **Putting off the wealth building program for five years could cost nearly half a million dollars.**

ANOTHER SECRET OF WEALTH

Unfortunately income tax can punch a hole in your plans because under our progressive tax system the rate of tax rises as your income does. However when you buy an asset such as property or shares any capital gain automatically becomes part of the current value without any action on your part. As a result the compounding process is automatic because no capital gains tax is payable until the asset is sold.

A clever way to wealth which is used by most serious investors is to borrow money for the asset and to pay the interest regularly instead of letting it compound. When they do this the asset value should grow faster and faster because of the compounding effect[2]. At the same time the debt will remain static and the investors equity (the difference between the asset value and the loan) will grow.

Imagine an investor bought a rental house for $100 000 using a deposit of $50 000 and a loan of $50 000. The deposit is called the investor's equity. If the interest on the loan was $5 000 a year and the rents from the house were $5 000 a year the investor could sit back and let the tenant pay the interest. If the house doubled in value in 10 years and the loan balance did not drop the investor would then have a $200 000 house with a $50 000 loan. The initial equity of $50 000 has grown to $150 000 (house value $200 000 less loan $50 000 = $150 000).

What has always fascinated me about compound interest is that it works in ways that seem totally illogical.

Think about two young people beginning separate investment programs for their retirement. The first starts putting $1 000 a year away at age 18 but stops at 30 to invest elsewhere. The second does not start till age 30 but then invests, without fail, $2 000 a year till age 65.

Who do you think will end up with the largest sum of money if the rate of return is 10% in each case?

Strange though it may seem the winner is the first one who contributed only $13 000 but ended up with $690 000. The loser is the one who delayed and finished with $542 000 for a total investment of $70 000.

I hope this lesson on compound interest has got you fired up and ready to go. Don't forget that it takes time to work and that you need money to use it. Our next lesson will show you how to make that money.

---

2. Naturally this assumes the asset will enjoy capital growth. If it falls in value the owner's loss is magnified.

22

HOW TO EARN MORE MONEY

*Everything you want in life has a price connected to it.
There's a price to pay if you want to make things better, a
price to pay for leaving things as they are.*

Harry Browne

In every country there is a massive gap between the income earned by the lowest and the highest paid people. In this chapter you'll learn why this is so and what is needed to put yourself in the higher income brackets.

Money is a medium that lets one person exchange goods and services for that of another. Therefore it should be obvious that the more goods or services **you** can **offer** the more money you are likely to **receive** in exchange. Yet some goods and services are worth more than others. A shop assistant provides services yet earns less for an hour's work than a teacher who may earn less than a plumber who in turn receives less than a doctor. Do you find this confusing? No one of these individuals is any better than any other and all fill essential roles in our community. Why the difference in remuneration?

Here is the formula; the amount of money you are paid depends on:

(1) The demand for your services.

(2) How well you do what you do.

(3) The difficulty in replacing you.

If you think about the above for a while you may decide that being very good at what you do is the area on which to concentrate. That is the one over which you have most control. Also, if you are particularly good at what you do, the other two will fall into place naturally because your services will be in demand and you will certainly be hard to replace.

A client of mine has a retail diamond and jewellery shop. When you walk into that shop a woman, Mary, stands out. She has a bright look in her eye, is always happy and smiling, knows all the regular customers by name and is a treat to deal with. I asked the owner recently how long she had been there. He replied "Over 10 years and she is priceless. If she left I could not replace her". I have no doubt Mary receives a far higher salary than most other shop assistants in this country and that she would be swamped with offers if she ever decided to leave her present job.

Now you may think this pay system is a bit unfair and believe the highest paid people should be school teachers or university lecturers because they have the responsibility of educating our next generation. You may feel doctors are most important because they can save lives and help bring babies into the world.

That might be fine in theory but in real life the system doesn't work like that. Your income is determined not by fairness but by the market. A popular author might write absolute garbage but will be highly paid if enough people like to read what he or she turns out. Some television stars may receive a huge amount of money for making five 30 minute appearances on the box every week, a sporting hero may earn a million dollars in one match, a rock group might receive more for a two-hour concert than most people earn for a year's work. That happens because there is a huge demand for their services and skills.

Think about the other side of that coin for it contains a valuable lesson for you. The majority of authors, TV workers, sports professionals and musicians are in the lowest paid ranks of the work force because so many people want to get into those "glamour" industries. They all want to make it big but only a tiny number reach the top. Those that do are at the absolute peak of their profession. They are the best at what they do – at least in the public eye.

All markets operate on the theory of supply and demand. The more people there are seeking the same kind of work, the less any one of them is likely to be paid. If you are a migrant with no specific skills and can hardly speak English you may well end up doing process work in a factory where you are in danger of being replaced by a robot. If you have spent your working life in an administrative job with the one organisation you may have trouble finding a job if you are retrenched at age 50 because a whole group of retrenched people are trying to find similar jobs in an area where the jobs are being replaced by technology.

It is often easier to find jobs if you are prepared to travel to remote areas because few people want to go there. A friend of mine is now aged 65 and his services as a cost accountant are still in high demand because he will work in places like Indonesia or Dubai.

Remote jobs usually pay more than the equivalent position in the city and saving is easier in those places because there is often little to spend your money on. Many clients of our firm got their financial start in life by working in the country or in one of those non-glamorous overseas areas. They set a goal to build up a large sum of investment capital and accomplished it by spending five years there and working long hours.

Now you understand that the employment market works on supply and demand you will appreciate the importance of improving your skills. This will help you to become a member of the select band whose skills are in demand instead of being just another member of a large group chasing any job you can get. The top people in their fields always have job security as well as higher than average incomes.

YOU'VE GOT TO PUT IN THE HOURS

Those of you who want to earn your money in a more conventional way will find it will all fall into place if you practise what I have taught you in this book. Throughout I have stressed the importance of self-development and going the extra mile because this will enable you to develop the skills to put you at the top of your chosen field. In the next chapter I will show you how to "multiply" yourself and move into the really high earning field by progressing toward having your own business. However, when you are starting off, there is just no substitute for putting in the time.

The good news is that when you find the right path for yourself the long hours don't matter because you will be enjoying what you do. I started writing this chapter at 4.45 on a Saturday morning in December, just a week before Christmas. We were holidaying at the beach and I was sitting with my portable computer on a patio looking over the surf. The rest of the family was sleeping peacefully but I couldn't think of anything I would rather be doing.

What if you don't like working long hours? Find a hobby you enjoy because you are on a lifelong holiday once you discover something to work at that you love doing. I have stressed there is no connection between money and happiness and you may have to settle for lower earnings if the field you enjoy does not return a huge income. If that is the case go for what you enjoy.

HOW TO SCORE A PROMOTION

Remember your rewards in life will match your service, therefore the more time you put into developing your skills and providing service the greater will be your rewards. Even if these rewards come in the form of personal satisfaction instead of money you will have a fulfilled life.

I'll now let you inside an employer's mind and show you how to carve a fast track up the ladder of success.

Let's pretend you are the owner of a small to medium sized business, you have just lost one of your key staff and you have to find a replacement.

You prefer a hassle-free existence like everybody else and two jobs you don't enjoy are hiring and firing people. You know that hiring is always a problem because if you use a personnel agency there are substantial fees to pay and if you decide to find the person yourself there is the

time consuming process of drafting the advertisements, screening all the applications, interviewing those who appear promising, making a final decision and then writing "sorry" letters to all those who missed out.

That can take weeks of your valuable time and after it's all been done there is no guarantee the person you chose will be right for the job. If he or she does prove to be unsuitable you have to start the whole time-consuming process all over again.

You know that firing a person is also difficult because few people are so bad that their behaviour warrants instant dismissal. Usually the performance is not quite as good as you hoped and despite counselling and training the feeling slowly but surely grows inside you that this person is not suited for the job. Finally you decide they should go but your emotions get in the way (it may be their first job or they may be supporting a family) and you keep putting it off. Eventually after several months of internal strain you take action or, if you are lucky, they leave and go elsewhere.

Wouldn't you be pleased to know there is another way to approach the problem and that it is used now by progressive companies such as McDonald's. That is to select the replacement from the ranks of your existing staff members if possible.

As the proverb says "The devil you know is better than the devil you don't" and you could save so much valuable time if you could look around your present staff to see if one of them is suitable. Naturally you would eliminate the stirrers, the late comers, those who spend half their time on personal phone calls and those who are more interested in themselves than your business. However, amongst your own people you will usually find that rare gem who does go the extra mile, who is keen to develop their skills and who is both competent and pleasant to work with. You might not give them the job immediately but you will offer it on a temporary basis to see how they handle it. Usually they do it well and then you have made two people happy, yourself and the staff member who got the promotion.

In most companies there are people leaving regularly. This happens for many reasons that may include transfer of a spouse, a decision to start a family, termination, travel overseas, ill health or a better offer elsewhere. If you do what I have taught you in this book you will be the one in the running for the promotion when the chance inevitably comes.

WHY EARN MORE MONEY?

We agree that it takes hard work and time to earn more money and many of you will be asking yourselves if the price is worth paying. Only you can answer that but I urge you to give the question more than a passing thought before you give a negative answer. What do you honestly feel deep down? Do you lack the drive to do what needs to be done or are you frightened that you will do all the work and still not get the rewards. Do you doubt your own ability?

These are complex questions but a way to help find the right answer for you is to ask yourself what you would do if you won ten million dollars today. If thoughts of a big home, exotic trips and expensive cars come to mind immediately you **do** have a desire for material things. Any lack of motivation on your part is due to your not knowing where to start or self doubt. By the time you finish this book you will know where to start and provided you make a start on your goals and your self-development program there is no reason why you should not succeed.

Remember that earning more money will assist you to do the things you want to do and have the things you want to have. It will also help you in three important areas:

(1) It will provide a higher standard of living so you will have more money to spend each week.

(2) You will have more money to invest which means you will attain financial independence at an earlier age.

(3) The skills you develop to earn the extra money will also assist you to reach your full potential which I believe is your duty. They will enable you to take advantage of many other valuable opportunities in the future.

The amount of money you **earn** is a reward for the service you give. The amount of money you **have** is a product of the techniques you use for retaining it and making it grow. Combine the skills of earning and investing it and financial independence is assured.

23

GO FOR PROFITS NOT WAGES

There is no security on this earth; there is only opportunity.

General Douglas MacArthur

If you've got this far you should be aware I believe a happy and successful life means you are in control of it. Now I'll explain why one of the best ways to be in control is for you to have your own business.

Now don't let your eyes glaze over and say "Who, me?". If you follow the principles in this book you will be way ahead of "most people" and ultimately you will be able to achieve any realistic goals you set. Therefore moving towards a position where you can start your own business should not be nearly as scary as it may sound.

A word of warning. I promised you a happy and fulfilled life, not one that was free of hassles. If you run a business you will be at the mercy of your customers, your staff, the bank manager, suppliers, economic cycles and every branch of government. However it's worth it. Having your own business means you can choose how much you want to be paid, what hours you work and when you want to have holidays. It is also one of the best ways to use the skills you have gained by personal development because you will succeed or fail on your merits.

136

Now if you are not too comfortable with the idea of succeeding or failing on your merits you have missed the whole point of this book. Let me repeat it. I believe human beings can **choose** success, that success is predictable and that success involves carrying out certain steps and it requires that you develop appropriate skills. If that is not true then it's all a matter of luck or being born to the right parents in which case we're all wasting our time trying to change what can't be changed.

Being in business means that you are providing a service that people want. It may be:

A factory to produce goods people need to use.

A security service to protect their homes.

A sports shop where they can buy clothes.

A garage where they can have their cars serviced.

An accounting service to help with tax and bookkeeping.

A real estate agency to help buyers and sellers of property.

A pest control service to keep their home free of insect pests.

A financial adviser to guide them with their investments.

A motel where they can stay when travelling.

A restaurant where they can eat.

A doctor to help the sick.

A builder to construct buildings.

I could fill up this book with different services but if you stop for a few minutes to browse through the Yellow Pages you may be amazed at the huge range of businesses that exist. In America now there are even businesses that will check your phone bill or baby-sit your pets.

You have probably heard an expression that is used in financial planning circles – "The higher the risk the higher the reward". It works for business too because going into business often involves taking risks. People in business usually work long hours and when they are starting off they take on commitments such as big mortgages and long leases. They do this for the rewards of more income, the freedom from working for a boss and for the glorious feeling of being able to say "This is my business and it will survive or perish because of my actions". They also face the possibility of losing everything they have if it goes bad.

LEARNING A LESSON

I learned that profits were better than wages when I was a young poverty-stricken bank officer aged 23 earning around $40 a week[1]. I had struck up a friendship that endures to this day with a larger than life character named Eric. He left school at 14 and worked as a shop assistant for a while but discovered that his lifestyle

---

1. This was before the introduction of decimal currency. I have converted the figures to dollars for ease of understanding.

needed more than a shop assistant's wages and promptly started selling real estate. My first memories of our friendship are of him spending each weekend sitting on a vacant estate waiting for buyers. You could see the ground through the rust holes in the floor of his car.

His hard work paid off and by the time he was 28 he owned several properties. One property was a commercial building that housed his own office as well as one of Brisbane's leading illegal gambling dens. We had been having a few drinks at Tattersalls Club where he is a member when Eric decided he would buy some cheese to take home to his wife. He handed over four dollars and we walked off with a huge round block of cheese. On the way home he decided to broaden my knowledge by taking me for a tour of the premises of his main tenant – the gambling den.

We walked up the stairs, pressed the buzzer, gave the right password and the huge solid steel door opened. I had expected an elegant atmosphere but found myself in a smoky room that was crammed with tables occupied by foreign-looking men in grubby working clothes. There were huge piles of bank notes on each table. Naturally the proprietor of this establishment was Louie and he was bemoaning the fact that he needed some snacks to keep his clients' minds off their stomachs and on the gambling. Eric announced he had a large cheese that would do the job perfectly. "Fine," said Louie. "How much?". Quick as a flash Eric came back with "Twenty dollars!!".

Louie happily pulled a twenty dollar note from the huge roll he had in his pocket and we were on our way. Eric had just made more in five minutes than I could make in two full days at the bank.

THE POWER OF MULTIPLYING YOURSELF

When you have your own business you can multiply your efforts by employing others. As you know most business people employ staff and when they are working out what to charge their customers they include the cost of materials, if appropriate, and also add a margin for staff wages and other overheads. The owner must make a profit out of the staff to cover the other costs of the business and to provide a profit. This is where the leverage comes in.

Imagine you are a top gardener and can earn $20 an hour. The most you can ever earn is the number of hours you work multiplied by $20. Even if you worked to the point of exhaustion for, say seven days a week for 10 hours a day, $1 400 a week is the limit of your income.

Imagine how much more you could earn if you had a team of people working for you and you were co-ordinating them to make the best use of their skills combined with yours. Maybe you are supervising the job and paying your gardeners $15 an hour, your labourers $10 an hour, your juniors $6 an hour and yet are still charging out the whole job at $20 an hour. You could increase your income still further by selling products such as plants, fertilisers, sleepers and soil and making a profit on those as well. Now your income is limited only by the size of the operation you can manage and not by the hours of physical work you can do.

The founders of the giant Amway Corporation are Rich De Vos and Jay van Andel. They are both qualified pilots and started their business careers by giving flying lessons.

Life changed for them when they discovered they could make far more money by selling flying lessons than by teaching people to fly. Once they had sold the lessons they hired other pilots to give them. They had learned the power of multiplying themselves.

A friend of mine started a language school by the simple process of placing advertisements for students in the travel section of the paper and advertisements for casual language teachers in the employment section. Once she had put together her team of casual teachers it was only a matter of co-ordinating classes. The pupils paid by the lesson and she paid the teachers by the hour.

USING YOUR INITIATIVE

My young friend and neighbour Ben has been mowing my lawns and helping me in the garden for the last few years. He was only ten when his father died tragically but this has not stopped his drive. He earned his first few dollars by mowing lawns and by finding and selling lost golf balls at the nearby golf course. When the land around us was cut up for development Ben noticed there were up to 60 workers on site at any one time. He recognised an opportunity and bought cases of soft drinks at wholesale prices, chilled them and sold them to the workers for a profit of 50 cents a can. He did this by pushing a huge wheelbarrow with an icebox full of drinks around the sites. As his sales increased he expanded his range to include chocolate bars and sandwiches (which he paid his mother to make for him).

Ben is a delightful young man but he has also acquired the habit of going the extra mile. We live on a four hectare property with a huge expanse of lawns and gardens and he is continually finding new areas that need a mow or a clip. I have no doubt he will be a success at whatever he decides to do.

I suggest you establish a little business of your own as soon as possible so as to start to gain an idea of what it takes. The skills needed to run a business include marketing, pricing, arranging supplies, doing what you promise and putting up with the whims of customers. If you like the idea of selling you could consider a multi level marketing operation such as Advanced Life Foods, Amway, Nutrimetics, Omegatrend or Tupperware to name just a few. Here you will gain invaluable experience and personal growth as well as making some useful pocket money[2].

If you don't find that appealing you could try some casual work in a small business. This may be at the local store, at the bottle shop or even delivering brochures. The type of work is not important at this stage for the purpose of doing it is to give you an insight into the way a business functions.

When you are thinking about a career now think about establishing your own business after a few years of being employed by somebody else. You will find many obvious fits. For example:

A police officer can start a security business.

A union official can become an industrial relations consultant.

A carpenter can become a builder.

A hotel employee may start a small restaurant.

Once you become experienced in your field you will find the opportunities will appear.

As this chapter comes to an end think again about the words of General Macarthur that started it off. *There is no security, only opportunity.* The 1990's will bring the most extraordinary opportunities for those who are prepared for them. If you can run your own business effectively in this climate the rewards will be there for the taking.

---

2. The names are listed in alphabetical order. There are many such reputable companies to consider.

24

THE TOOLS OF THE TRADE

All our dreams can come true if we have the courage to pursue them.

Walt Disney

In this chapter I will describe the tools you need to manage your money efficiently.

There is little doubt you will be well off financially if you follow what you have learned by reading this book but life will be easier if you establish a system to handle your money properly. You already know how to prepare a budget but I will now show you the mechanics of dealing with your money as it flows in and out.

You will need:

(1) A cheque account.

(2) A credit or debit card.

(3) A cash book.

THE CHEQUE ACCOUNT

Keeping track of your money will be easier if all your money transactions pass through an all purpose cheque account. This is an account into which you bank your pay as well as any other income you receive and from which you make all your payments.

Before you select a cheque account shop around the

143

banks, building societies and credit unions and select one that pays interest and has low or even nil bank fees (all accounts suffer government taxes) for keeping the account. It can be confusing because often the interest paid to you is lower if the account fees are low and in other cases you have to keep your balance over a certain figure, such as $500, to enjoy freedom from fees.

The main purpose of a cheque account is convenience because you can pay a bill by writing out a cheque and sending it to a person to whom you owe money. Your time is valuable and mailing a cheque saves waiting time travelling to where the money is due and then standing in line to pay it. Another benefit is that you have a record of the payment and to facilitate this I suggest you write the invoice number on the cheque butt. Also write the cheque number and the date paid on your copy of the invoice. You will then have a complete record and it will save time if you happen to be selected for a tax audit.

Keeping good records will prove invaluable if someone wrongly claims you owe them money. All you have to do is verify the transaction with your cheque butt and bank statement and tell the creditor when the cheque was paid by your bank.

If you use a cheque account for all your transactions you will have a record of all your receipts and payments and it will be easy to balance your income and expenditure with your budget. This is why it is better to ask for a large deposit book and a large cheque book. Small ones are easily lost and there is plenty of room in the larger ones to write in extra information.

For many of you the only income item will be your salary but the expenses will be far greater in number and more diverse. Provided you pay them all from your cheque account you will find that over a year or so a spending pattern will emerge. This information will be invaluable when you come to review your budget.

DEBIT/CREDIT CARDS

I usually suggest avoiding credit cards because they can lure you into debt, but they are so convenient that you should consider their use in the right circumstances. Understand there are two types of cards: debit cards and credit cards. A **debit card** enables you to withdraw from your account without writing a cheque. For example if your salary goes directly into your cheque account you will find it is a simple matter to go to an automatic teller machine, insert your debit card and withdraw $100 or so for spending. It can also be used at many retail outlets whereby you hand over your card and the cost of the item is immediately deducted from your account.

The great feature about debit cards is that you do not have to waste time in a queue at the bank waiting to cash a cheque. Also you cannot be enticed into living beyond your means by spending money you don't have because there is no provision for you to borrow.

Credit cards look the same as debit cards and are somewhat similar in the way they work. The main difference is that you are given a limit (say $2 000) up to which you can spend. The payments are not automatically debited to your bank account. Instead, each month you receive a statement detailing what you owe. When the credit card statement arrives you have the choice of paying the whole balance owing or paying at least 5% of the outstanding balance and leaving the remainder of the debt there as a loan at a high rate of interest.

You should now understand how credit cards can get you into trouble. Think about two people we'll call Doug and Sam. Each of them owed $800 on his credit card statement when it arrived. Doug paid the whole balance but Sam decided to pay back only $40 and leave $760 owing. Sam now should have $760 more than Doug does in his cheque account but has to pay the interest on the $760 still outstanding. He also has greater buying power than Doug because he has the $760 that he did not use to pay his debts as well as any undrawn balance on the credit card. If Sam lacks discipline he may go out and buy more and start the dangerous habit of living on credit.

Which card should you use? Both if you have willpower; a debit card only if you haven't. When you are making cash withdrawals a debit card is far more convenient than cashing a cheque and the use of a credit card for purchases enables you to have up to a month's grace (depending on the card) before you have to pay for them. During this time you have the use of the money and can earn interest on it.

THE CASH BOOK

Don't be worried by the term cash book. It is only a book that is ruled up in such a way as will help you keep track of your income and expenses. All you have to do is keep one page for income and one page for expenditure and list each item in order. When you come to the end of the month or the end of the quarter, you can total the columns and obtain a complete analysis of all your spending. No longer will you say in frustration "I have no idea where my money goes".

If you are the type that can't be bothered keeping detailed records such as a cash book you can also get the information by listing the totals onto a sheet of paper directly from your cheque butts and deposit book duplicates. You should insist on receiving regular statements of your cheque account and you may find a simple way to keep track of your spending is to write the payee of each cheque next to the entry on the statement.

If you get into the habit of keeping accurate records and watching your budget you will soon find your money starting to build up. The next chapter will tell you what to do with it.

25

INVESTMENTS TO GET YOU GOING

Ideas are the beginning points of all fortunes.
Napoleon Hill

This chapter will point you towards the investments that are best suited for a younger person starting off on the road to financial independence.

You now understand the principles of building wealth and the importance of making other people's money work for you by careful borrowing. You know the harm that comes if you fall into the trap of becoming a slave to others by getting bogged down in a mire of borrowing for items that have no lasting value. You have made a good start on the road to success.

Throughout this book I have stressed the importance of ongoing self-development and that taking the time to improve your skills is the best investment you can make. However this will almost certainly lead to your having plenty of money so we'll now move on to the subject of wise investing. *Making Money Made Simple* contains the information in detail but this chapter will give you a brief summary to start you off.

There may appear to be a dazzling array of investment opportunities around but almost every investment falls into one of two categories – debt investments or equity investments.

When you make a **debt investment** you deposit money with an establishment such as a bank, building society or credit union who in turn lend it out to people who wish to borrow it. Your return is solely from the interest you receive.

When you make an **equity investment** you invest it in areas such as real estate, shares, gold or antiques. It changes character and in some cases you may receive income (rent for property, dividends from shares) and also some capital gain.

Which category is right for you? That depends on what you are trying to achieve. There is no perfect investment that will be all things to all people so don't waste your time looking for it. Instead take the time to understand the good and bad points of each type of investment so you will be able to choose the ones that are best for you.

DEBT INVESTMENTS

The most common form of debt investment is a bank account. When you put $2 000 in the bank you can be fairly certain that when you come to withdraw it the $2 000 will still be there plus whatever interest it may have earned in the meantime. As a rule there are no charges when you deposit or withdraw but there may be bank fees for keeping the account as well as those irritating small taxes the government levies on the account.

The advantages are the certainty of the money being there when you need it, the lack of costs for depositing and withdrawing, and the ability to withdraw all or part of it at short notice.

There are two disadvantages. The first is that you are liable to pay tax on the interest and the rate of this tax will rise as your other income rises. The second is the lack of capital growth. Money is only worth what it can buy and each year this is reduced by inflation. If you left that $2 000 in the bank for five years you may find that it would buy far less than it would buy now. This is called inflation and if you want to see it in practice go to the library and browse through some old newspapers. You will be amazed at the prices of everything.

EQUITY INVESTMENTS

There are many equity investments but the most common are real estate or shares. There are two major advantages. One is that you have the chance to receive a higher return overall than you would if you left your money in the bank because you may receive capital gain as well as income. The other advantage is that the tax on the capital gain is taxed at a lower rate than income tax. This tax is called capital gains tax. It is not due until the investment is sold and even then is reduced to take inflation into account.

The disadvantages are possible costs to invest or to get your money back and the chance of your money dropping in value.

Let's imagine you had saved up $5 000 for a trip you wanted to take next year and you decided to buy shares because you had heard there was a boom about to happen and there were bundles of money to be made. If you invested the $5 000 in shares you would have to pay the stock broker around $150 (3%) when you bought them which has reduced your original capital by 3% immediately. There is a further 3% to pay when you sell but the dollar amount of this will depend on the selling price. If you struck it lucky and they rose to $6 000 (a 20% gain) the selling brokerage would be $180. Thus your total buying and selling costs are $330 or 6.6% of the initial value.

If the shares had stayed around their original value you would still have been liable for brokerage of $150 when you sold them. That's equal to 6% of your original capital. Unless the shares gain in value by 6% you have not even come out square and would have done much better by leaving your money in the bank.

The other problem with equity investments is

highlighted by the axiom "Wherever there is a chance of a capital gain there is a chance of a capital loss". What if the market slumped suddenly as happened in the 1987 stock market crash and the value of your shares dropped by 30% or more. You could find that your $5 000 had dwindled to not much more than $ 3 500.

Real estate and share investments should be the foundation of any long term investment portfolio and I am not highlighting their disadvantages to put you off placing money in these areas. Nevertheless it is important you understand they should only be used in the right circumstances and that placing money in these areas is a long term project.

Most young people have the savings goals of a car, a house and travel. In many cases the money for these is best placed in the interest bearing area. However, depending on the time frame, a regular savings plan through a balanced unit trust can be appropriate.

A balanced unit trust is a pool of money, managed by a fund manager, that is invested in both debt and equity investments. The fund would normally have its money invested in interest-bearing accounts, government bonds, local and overseas shares and real estate. Investments in these are made through licensed financial advisers.

SOME IMPORTANT RULES FOR THE YOUNGER INVESTOR

(1) **Never enter into an investment that requires a contract from you to enter into a savings plan for a period of years.** These "investments" are usually peddled for the sole purpose of providing a high commission to the person flogging them.

Don't confuse these with schemes where you sign an authority to have X dollars a month taken from your bank account and invested into a unit trust or a special savings account. These are fine because you can stop or change the amount or timing of the payments without penalty. They are among the best ways of saving you can use.

A good way to check the bona fides of the investment is to ask if there are any penalties if you decide to stop after six months or wish to withdraw some or all of your money then. If there are penalties for doing this don't sign up. The best way to protect yourself if you are told there are no penalties is to insist for written confirmation that this is true.

(2) **Stay right away from additional superannuation.** If you are working your employer should have enrolled you in the work scheme and this is all you need at this stage in your life. Any money you place in superannuation now is likely to be locked up until you turn 60. That may be 40 years away. Do you really want to tie up money for that long?

(3) Shop around for **safe high interest savings accounts** such as are offered by some building societies and credit unions. Younger people are usually saving for a car, a trip

or a house deposit and the appropriate place for this money is a debt type investment. The term of such a savings goal is usually less than three years and you do not want to lose money through fees or through drops in the market. Shopping around will teach you skills that will come into their own when you start looking for that first home loan.

(4) If you can take a long term view **don't be scared to put some of your money into shares or share based investments** such as equity trusts. Try to add to the investment regularly and make sure you re-invest all your dividends. You'll be amazed how it will grow but bear in mind that you should be prepared to leave the money untouched for at least five years. This strategy is suitable for a 20-year-old who has a goal to buy a house at 25.

(5) **Be wary of pooling your money with others to buy a house.** It might seem a good idea at the outset but people's circumstances change and one of your co-owners might be retrenched or transferred and want the property sold at a bad time. If you are keen to buy a property save a deposit and then speak to a lending institution. They are the best business partners you can have because, provided you make the monthly payments, they will leave you alone.

(6) If you now owe money on credit cards or personal loans your best investment is to cancel the credit cards and **concentrate on paying off any outstanding debts** as quickly as possible. This will save you hundreds of dollars in interest which you can invest elsewhere.

(7) You will probably find that a **no fee cheque account coupled with a high interest savings account** is the best place for your surplus money. This combines the convenience of writing cheques with the advantage of earning extra interest to boost you along the road to wealth.

(8) **Put off buying a car for as long as you can.** It has been estimated that owning a car costs over $100 a week which is a massive amount to come out of a low earner's

budget. If it is possible and practical live at home and use the family car.

(9) **Don't rush into buying a block of land or a house** until you have thoroughly researched the market and you know value when you see it. If you intend borrowing for the purchase wait until you have saved a substantial deposit so as to reduce your interest costs.

(10) Ensure you keep **separate** special purpose accounts for events such as holidays, buying a car or Christmas. Doing this ensures the money is available for the special purpose when needed. It also prevents you falling into the trap of overspending that can occur if you mix your special purpose money with your other funds.

If you follow these 10 rules you should be laying a sound foundation for your future wealth. **Remember that managing your money well is more important than the amount you earn** and that the best investment you can make is to develop your skills. Ensure your personal budget contains provision for books, audio tapes and training courses.

26

GETTING IT
TOGETHER

*A mind stretched to a new idea never goes back to its
original dimensions.*
Oliver Wendell Holmes

When I put down *Think and Grow Rich* I knew my life
could never be the same again. It was as if a veil had
been lifted from my eyes and I could suddenly see clearly
for the first time. My wish is that you will be now feeling
this way too for if you can start to look at yourself and life
in a fresh way you are well on the road to success.

Treat this book as a key that has opened the gate to a
new path. For a while you will be like a foal on wobbly
legs as you take those first hesitant steps along the way.
You will fall over, you will face set-backs, and often things
won't happen as you planned. However you will slowly
make progress as the habits of success take over your
thinking. Like compound interest that progress will
gather speed as time passes.

There is no doubt the future will present extraordinary
opportunities to those who are prepared. Technology will
continue to boom requiring highly skilled people to
maintain the machines and write the software. Travel and
its associated industries such as accommodation and
restaurants will be crying out for good staff while the
most competent people in the building trades area will be

sought after. There will continue to be break-throughs in science and medicine and many openings will appear for work with ageing people. As ever, top marketing people will be prized. There will be a strong demand for financial advisers, accountants and lawyers as regulations and laws become more complex. There will not be enough **good** people about to fill the vacancies.

Let's cast our minds back on what you have read to date. I started by saying I was concerned by the lack of confidence being felt by young people but pointed out that you face a unique set of challenges that also provide great opportunities for those who know how to handle them. The aim of the book is to release the potential you have inside you so as to enable you to handle these new challenges.

In the first three chapters I described the potential in all of us and tried to help you define what success is for you. Certainly success means different things to different people and you must find your own path.

We moved into the problem areas in the next chapter when I introduced the concept of "most people". They are the majority who go through life wishing and hoping things will change but never do anything positive about it except buy Lotto tickets. If you choose to live in the ranks of "most people" you will waste your life dreaming instead of achieving.

In chapter five I showed you the magic formula that can start a chain reaction. It starts with a belief, which will begin moving to reality when you write down the goal. However a goal without a plan to carry it through is nothing more than a wish. Only by making plans and taking action can you get what you want.

In chapters six and seven I introduced you to the idea of reframing and to the notion of a self-concept. Undoubtedly how we see ourselves has a huge effect on our performance but we live in a generally negative world where our brains are bombarded from birth with negative images. The way to improve the self-concept is to slowly form the habit of achieving little successes so that each small success gives you the confidence to try the next one. Eventually you will start to think of yourself as a person who can solve your own problems instead of being a victim in a world over which you have no control.

The law of sowing and reaping is such an obvious one that you would wonder why it needs to be mentioned at all. Yet "most people" spend their lives trying to reap the crop without planting the seed. Consequently as Thoreau said "the mass of men lead lives of quiet desperation[1]" .

In chapters nine and ten I discussed the importance of goal setting and gave you three essential skills to speed your journey on the road to success. These are getting into the habit of going the extra mile, gaining some basic sales skills and learning to speak in public. A person who can do these three things has jumped into the top five per cent of the population because so few will even attempt them.

Chapter 11 repeats the theme of the book – in order to have more you must become more. We should think of life as a continual "do it yourself" process.

Chapter 12 contains the vital but perhaps sad message that we must fail in order to succeed for the only way to increase our value is to learn new skills. Every new skill takes pain and effort. Hence the expression "No gain without pain". Throughout the book I have described some of my own negative thoughts to help you understand that it is normal to have fears and normal to make mistakes. One of my problems when I was young was thinking that nobody but me had fears or made mistakes.

The next chapter stressed the importance of having a positive mental attitude. It is well documented that those who think in positive terms achieve positive results and that a positive mental attitude is an essential attribute of a winner.

I continued in this vein by urging you to try as many new experiences as possible so as to speed up your personal development. Next came the universal laws which may have appeared strange to you at first as they are concerned with opposites. To receive you first have to give, and often your best successes come out of your failures.

By this stage you were two-thirds through the book and the lessons turned to finance, because money plays such a large part in our society. There is no doubt that nothing can take the place of money in the areas where money works. These include giving you access to a better education, a higher standard of living and the ability to make more choices in your life.

A knowledge of interest is essential because the proper use of interest will allow you to speed up the wealth-creation process while an over-reliance on interest has put many people in bankruptcy. I let you into the secret of compound interest and showed you why it is important to manage your money so as to build a capital base. The best way to do this is to use a budget which ensures that every dollar is put to its best use. In chapter 23 I urged you to consider steps that would lead to you having your own business as this was the best way to increase your income. The book finished by discussing the range of investments that are suitable for the person who is starting off.

As we finish understand that your brain is like your body. It needs regular food and exercise to function effectively. If this book is to be of lasting value you will have to regard it as the starting point on your road to success and continue to learn more about the subject. The Success Library and the hints for effective reading in Appendix 1 will help you.

I think now may be an appropriate time to take a break and reflect on a little poem a friend of mine showed me as she was reading the manuscript. Unfortunately its origins are unknown.

There is an older person up there ahead of you, that you ought to know
That person looks like you, talks like you, walks like you
That person has your eyes, your nose, your chin and

*whether he or she hates you or loves you, respects you or
despises you or is hungry or comfortable depends on you.
You made that person.*

That is you: ten years, twenty years, thirty years from now.

Anon

This is the final chapter in this book but I hope it will be
the start of a new life for you., I can do no more than wish
you good health and happiness as you go out there and
start getting it all together.

APPENDIX ONE

BUILDING A SUCCESS LIBRARY

You are the same today as you will be in five years except for two things, the people you meet and the books you read.

Charles E. Jones

Whenever I write, I think about a person I once met when I was doing a "book signing". Book signing involves sitting at a table in a busy street outside a book store autographing copies of your books for those who wish to buy them. To help attract a crowd the store may hire a publicity person who, with the aid of a microphone and a large loud-speaker, tries to entice passersby to stop and browse through the stacks of your books that cover the table. Occasionally a large group may gather around but more often almost everybody scurries by without giving you a second look.

The book signing I particularly remember took place at noon in Brisbane when I was signing copies of *Making Money Made Simple*. A young man walking by stopped to look at the book. He carried a pie and a can of Coke and he had a packet of cigarettes stuffed into a pocket on his sleeve. Obviously he worked on a nearby building site and there was an openness about him that appealed to me immediately.

He looked me up and down, put down the Coke, and

picked up one of my books. Then he said with a smile "Do you reckon I could read this?". "Yes, I reckon you could read it" I replied. We had a bit of a chat about earning and spending money and then he carried the book to the counter to pay for it. As he left he said "You know, I've never read a book."

Can you imagine how I felt? Jim Rohn had taught me *We are all affected by the books we haven't read* and I am a fervent believer in the power of books to change lives.[1]

I thought "What a responsibility I have. If he reads that book it may well change his life. Even if it doesn't, it might encourage him to read other books that may be of great help to him. If he finds my book boring, or heavy going, he probably won't finish it. Worse still, he may never pick up another book again."

Now you know why I write the way I do. Whenever I am reviewing what I have written I see that young man in my mind and think "Will he understand this?".

Just as a car needs petrol so does your mind need continual doses of motivation and knowledge. This book will show you where the road starts but it will be of little lasting benefit to you unless you keep widening your knowledge.

THE POWER OF BOOKS

You have probably had older people say to you "I wish I was your age and knew what I know now". Well, **you** won't need to say that when you're their age because you have access to much of the knowledge that older people have taken a lifetime to accumulate. Through books and other material such as video and audio tapes you **can** be young **and** know what they know now.

You can tap into some of the greatest minds that ever lived merely by going to a library or a book store. At one stage Og Mandino, who is now a famous writer, had bought a $30 revolver and was about to kill himself.

---

1. *Challenge to Succeed* Seminar by James Rohn.

However, something inside him made him pause and search for answers instead. He writes:

> I was just about as complete a failure as one can become. I began to spend a good deal of time in libraries looking for some answers. Where had I gone wrong? Was it too late for me? I found all the answers I needed in that golden vein of ore that every library has, that special shelf of books devoted to success, how to achieve it and how to hold on to it after one attains it. My counsellors were some of the wisest people who ever lived . . . people like Elbert Hubbard, Norman Vincent Peale, W. Clement Stone, Napoleon Hill, Dale Carnegie, Maxwell Maltz, Louis Binstock and Dorethea Brande. The advice from their books helped to change my life.[2]

In this section I will show you how to start a success library by recommending six books to start you off. Once you have finished these you may be ready to search around and find other books you enjoy and which will help you on your path to success. I have also included an Advanced List which contains some of my favourites and you may benefit from these too. Once you get into the habit of reading books and listening to audio tapes you will quickly discover what works for you and what doesn't.

In compiling the basic list I am conscious of my friend from the building site, and have picked six starter books that are easy to read and that are packed with useful information. Don't buy them all at once. Go to a good bookstore, browse through them and buy the one that feels right for you at the time. When you have read that one buy another. When you have read all six books you will probably be ready for a break and should look out for some good autobiographies.

---

2. Jones C.T. *Books You Read*. 1985:9. Executive Books, Harrisburg. PA.

HOW TO READ

Earlier in this book I mentioned the Buddhist saying *When the pupil is ready the teacher will appear*. Just reading this book has taken you to a new level of awareness and you will find if you read it again you will understand it better because a different you is the reader. This "new you" will look at life in a different light and see things you hadn't seen before. The higher awareness you have achieved will enable you to understand more of life in general. And your awareness will grow still further as you continue the learning process.

Find a book store or library in which you feel comfortable and get to know the staff there. They will be able to guide you into areas of special interest and suggest books and authors who may appeal to you.

Understand the awareness-growing process I mentioned above and appreciate that a book that doesn't seem right today may well contain the answers you need in the future. When you start to put together your own library you will be amazed what will happen as you progress through life. You will be able to go to your library, select a book at random and find it contains just the answer to your problem.

When you are choosing books watch the best seller lists in the newspapers and also look inside the front cover of a book to find the number of times it has been reprinted. If a book has been selling continually for years it is obvious that people are buying it and recommending it to their friends.

THE BASIC LIST

SEEDS OF GREATNESS by Denis Waitley. 236 pages. Approximate price $15. Published by Cedar. First published in Great Britain 1985. This book will build on many of the principles in *Getting it Together*.

THE RICHEST MAN IN BABYLON by George Clason. 144 pages. Approximate price $8. Published by Bantam, New York. First published 1926. The classic book on money that has been on the best seller lists for over 60 years.

THE GREATEST MIRACLE IN THE WORLD by Og Mandino. 110

pages. Approximate price $9. Published by Bantam, New York. First published 1970. This book has sold over five million copies. When you read it you will know why.

STRATEGIES OF THE CHAMPIONS by Vicki Peterson. 222 pages. Approximate price $14. Published by Pan Books, Sydney. First published 1988. This book is written from a sporting aspect but covers the principles of goal setting, mind control and mental and physical fitness.

MAKING MONEY MADE SIMPLE by Noel Whittaker. 324 pages. Approximate price $20. Published by Simon and Schuster. First published 1987. This covers the principles of finance, tax and investment and follows naturally from *Getting it Together*.

POWER TO CHOOSE by Haydn Sargent. 160 pages. Approximate price $13. Published by Boolarong Publications, Brisbane. First published 1989. This is a simple book which will help reinforce your self-concept.

THE ADVANCED LIST

PERSONAL DEVELOPMENT

AWAKEN THE GIANT WITHIN by Anthony Robbins. 538 pages. Approximate price $20. Published by Fireside, a division of Simon and Schuster. First published 1991.

THE 7 HABITS OF HIGHLY EFFECTIVE PEOPLE by Stephen Covey. 340 pages. Approximate price $20. Published by The Business Library, Melbourne. First published 1990.

THINK AND GROW RICH by Napoleon Hill. 254 pages. Approximate price $10. Published by Fawcett Crest, New York. First published 1937.

UNIVERSITY OF SUCCESS by Og Mandino. 526 pages. Approximate price $20. Published by Bantam, New York. First published 1982.

WORK SMARTER NOT HARDER by Jack Collis and Michael Le Boeuf. 236 pages. Approximate price $25. Published by Goal Getting Seminars, Sydney. First published 1992.

YOU'LL SEE IT WHEN YOU BELIEVE IT by Dr Wayne Dyer. 288 pages. Approximate price $15. Published by William Morrow and Company Inc, New York. First published 1989.

MONEY AND FINANCE

BUILDING WEALTH THROUGH INVESTMENT PROPERTY by Jan Somers. 190 pages. Approximate price $25. Published by Somerset Financial Services, Brisbane. First published 1992.

IN YOUR INTEREST by Peter Freeman. 252 pages. Approximate price $15. Published by Arrow Books. First published 1989.

MORE MONEY WITH NOEL WHITTAKER by Noel Whittaker. 376 pages. Approximate price $20. Published by Simon and Schuster. First published 1990.

HANDLING YOURSELF AND OTHERS

HOW TO STOP WORRYING AND START LIVING by Dale Carnegie. 304 pages. Approximate price $15. Published by Cedar. First published 1953.

LEARNED OPTIMISM by Martin Seligman. 320 pages. Approximate price $18. Published by Random House, Sydney. First published 1991.

WHY AM I AFRAID TO TELL YOU WHO I AM by John Powell. 166 pages. Approximate price $10. Published by Argus Communications, Chicago. First published 1969.

PSYCHO-CYBERNETICS by Maxwell Maltz. 282 pages. Approximate price $10. Published by Pocket Books, a division of Simon and Schuster. First published 1960.

SUCCESS THROUGH A POSITIVE MENTAL ATTITUDE by Napoleon Hill and W. Clement Stone, 254 pages. Approximate price $15. Published by Cornstalk Publishing, Sydney. First published 1960.

SALESMANSHIP

HOW TO MASTER THE ART OF SELLING by Tom Hopkins. 364 pages. Approximate price $13. Published by Grafton (Harper Collins) London. First published 1980.

You will notice the total cost of all the books listed above is less then $350. Just think about it. If you invested only three dollars a week for two years you'd be able to buy each of these books. You would then have one of the best success libraries in the country containing information that may be worth millions of dollars to you. It is also an asset that won't wear out and one that will bring you increasing joy as the years pass.

Many of the people who write to me say "Your books have changed my life but I wish I had read this material 30 years ago". You have a head start because the material is ready and waiting for you. All you have to do is read it.

INDEX

Whittaker Macnaught Pty Ltd
Level 5, Santos House
215 Adelaide Street
BRISBANE Q. 4000
TELEPHONE (07) 221 1022
FAX (07) 221 9682

Dear Reader

If you enjoyed *Getting it Together* you should broaden your knowledge by reading other books by Noel Whittaker. If you would like to be contacted when new editions are released please complete the form below and return it to us. We will then advise you when a new edition is due out and let you know details of the changes — you can then decide if you wish to purchase it.

Noel Whittaker's lectures on finance are in **great demand.** To help as many people as possible, Noel has released, on audio cassette, **a live recording** of his last 10-hour course to a class of 60. If you would like more details of this **outstanding educational opportunity** please tick the section in the coupon below.

Remember "Lack of knowledge can be very costly."

NO STAMP IS REQUIRED

REPLY PAID 386

Whittaker Macnaught Pty Ltd
GPO Box 2571
BRISBANE Q. 4001

☐ Please mail me details of "Noel Whittaker Live in the Lecture Room".

☐ Please advise me when updated editions of *Getting it Together, Making Money Made Simple* and *More Money with Noel Whittaker* are being released.

☐ Please advise discounts for bulk buying.

NAME...

ADDRESS...

....

....POSTCODE...............................